Thyssen-Bornemisza Collection
Villa Favorita

Elisabeth Storm Nagy

Europe and America 19th and 20th Century Paintings and Watercolours from the Thyssen-Bornemisza Collection

Guide to Exhibited Works

Fondazione
Thyssen-Bornemisza
Electa

Cover Illustration
Lucian Freud *Portrait of*
Baron H.H. Thyssen-Bornemisza
(Man in a Chair), 1983-85
Cat. No. 84

Photography:
Giuseppe Pennisi, Lugano

Filmsetting of the text
and reproduction of the
illustrations by
Bassoli-Olivieri Prestampa, Milan

Practical Information:

The present volume is intended as a guide for the general public. When relevant, the information contained herein has been based on the following scholarly catalogues in the sixteen-volume series on the Thyssen-Bornemisza Collection, published by Philip Wilson, London:
Barbara Novak, *Nineteenth-Century American Painting*, 1986
Gail Levin, *Twentieth-Century American Painting*, 1987
Peter Vergo, *Twentieth-Century German Painting*, 1992
And currently in preparation: John E. Bowlt and Nicoletta Misler, *Russian and East European Works*

The works included in this catalogue have been divided into two sections:
19th Century American Paintings, and 20th Century European and American Paintings and Watercolours. Within each section the paintings are listed alphabetically according to artist.

Acknowledgements:

The author wishes to extend a heartfelt thanks to the following for their invaluable assistance in the preparation of this catalogue, and in the mounting of this exhibition:

Emil Bosshard
John E. Bowlt
Lucia Cassol
Francesca von Habsburg
Anne G. Manning
Irene Martin
Marcello Mazzoleni
Salvatore Migliardi
Nicoletta Misler
Graziella Ombroni
Adriano Pierobon
Ursula Stevens
Ira Spanierman
Floriana Vismara

Also thanks to:
Robert L. Genillard
Sheldon Gordon
Istvan Nagy
Peter Istvan Nagy

Table of Contents

Foreword

The Villa Favorita opens its doors again to the public after being closed in 1992 for one of the most important art transfers ever. Over eight hundred paintings and works of art were carefully packed and shipped to Madrid where they are on view in a renovated palace, now called the Museo Thyssen-Bornemisza. The renovation of the gallery of the Villa Favorita began as the Madrid museum opened; it was the first major renovation since the construction of the gallery in 1936.

The gallery of Villa Favorita was originally built to house a private collection of Old Master paintings, and now it houses a collection of nineteenth- and twentieth-century works. The walls are a bright warm grey, giving the rooms a light and airy atmosphere, symbolically signifying the beginning of a new era for the Villa Favorita.

There are several reasons for choosing from the collection this particular group of nineteenth- and twentieth-century works for installation: These works have never been seen at the Villa Favorita; they complement the new, modern and more dynamic Villa Favorita; and they reflect the trans-Atlantic nature of the collection, *Europe and America*. Upon entry, the visitor is faced with a juxtaposition of the old and the new; the old architecture and the modern paintings, the Old World and the New World, yet they fit together comfortably. The second floor has been painted a modern white and hung with twentieth-century paintings, but furnished with antiques from the collection. A Florentine wall bench from circa 1550 is available for visitors to rest and contemplate the late fifteenth-century *Bust of a Young Woman* by Gian Cristoforo Romano which is flanked by a Vorticist painting by William P. Roberts entitled *Dock Gates* and a late abstract painting by Gino Severini, *Ritmo di pas de deux all'Opéra*. From time to time, these works will change. But the juxtaposing of this unexpected combination of works to stimulate the eye and mind in order to see new aspects within the works will continue.

The gallery has always been arranged in chronological order from the oldest to the most recent. Now the visitor will be challenged to see and think in reverse; to step backwards in time rather than looking for the next step forward to the present. The most recent or contemporary paintings are located in the first room and the earliest nineteenth century American paintings hang in the last which retains its original Venetian silk covered walls. Throughout the gallery, the visitor will be confronted with developments in Europe and America; movements in Europe and uniquely American movements placed, room by room, in this backward chronology. The last two rooms are dedicated to American nineteenth-century painting. The Thyssen-Bornemisza Collection is the only European collection to contain works from this period of American art. We feel that it is important to give the European visitors the opportunity to see these works, which up to now have only been available in Europe through temporary exhibitions.

This guide has been ably written by Elisabeth Storm Nagy in a catalogue style to give more than cursory information to the visitor. The entries, however, are not meant to be fully documented catalogue entries. For those interested in a catalogue raisonné, the Philip Wilson Publications series on the Thyssen- Bornemisza Collection is available (12 of a 16 to 18 volume series have been published). The extended entries for this guide book were deemed necessary due to the unfamiliarity of many artists, especially the Americans, to most visitors.

I wish the visitor a pleasant and informative tour of the collection with this guide book in hand.

Irene Martin
Administrative Director and Curator

Brief History of the
Thyssen-Bornemisza Collection

My father, Baron Heinrich Thyssen-Bornemisza (1875-1947), began to collect works by old master painters at the beginning of the 1920s. At that time my parents, who had been forced by the Communist Regime of Béla Kun to abandon their Castle Rohoncz in Hungary, were living in Holland, where I was born in 1921. My father was a successful financier and banker, who was very interested in art. The time up until World War II was ideal for collecting. During the twenties and thirties many great masterpieces were in private hands, and available at prices which were still reasonably affordable. Initially, my father bought paintings of the early German school (Hans Holbein the Younger, Albrecht Dürer, Albrecht Altdorfer, Hans Baldung Grien, Lucas and Hans Cranach), but also the Early Netherlandish school (Jan van Eyck and Hans Memling). With the advice of the legendary art dealer Rudolf Heinemann, my father was able to acquire outstanding Italian masterpieces during the 1930s by artists such as Domenico Ghirlandaio, Vittore Carpaccio and Caravaggio. He also widened the scope of the Collection to include sculptures, furniture, carpets, tapestries, mediaeval ivories, European goldsmith's work, and other decorative arts. When in 1932 it became necessary to find adequately large and safe housing for the expanding number of art treasures, my father bought the Villa Favorita on the shores of Lake Lugano, in the Swiss Canton of Ticino. The Villa dates back to the seventeenth century and has extensive gardens and terraces sloping down to the shores of the lake. It had been the property of various patrician families of Lugano until Prince Frederick Leopold of Prussia bought it in 1919. The prince enlarged the villa, known since the early nineteenth century as "Villa Favorita", and connected it with the existing Glorietta. The Prince also planted the cypresses along the lakefront. When my father bought it he restored the gardens and the various buildings on the property. In 1934, work started on a private gallery to be built adjacent to the Villa, designed by the architect Giovanni Geiser. The gallery had over twenty rooms to house the different schools of painting. It was luxuriously finished in fine marbles, and hung with Venetian silks and velvets. A corridor—a former library—connected the Villa with the Glorietta of the Gallery so my father could easily walk over and enjoy his treasures in peace and privacy. The war brought an end to my father's activities as a collector. After dedicating the whole collection—some 525 paintings—to his father August Thyssen, he bequeathed more than half of it to me, his youngest son. I inherited it on his death in 1947. The rest of the collection was broken up and divided among the other heirs. I had completed my studies in Switzerland during the war years. When my father died, I immediately set myself the goal of buying back the paintings distributed to my sisters and brother, so as to bring the Collection back to its original state. In 1948, I was able to open the Gallery to the public. From that time to the present I have continued to supplement the Collection of Old Masters, which now represents a broad panorama of the history of European painting, and includes the most important artists from the twelfth to the nineteenth century. I still buy Old Master paintings whenever I have the opportunity to enrich the Collection. I recently bought John Constable's *The Lock*, and have also expanded the section of Dutch and Flemish followers of Caravaggio. Since 1960, I have been acquiring art of the nineteenth and twentieth centuries, which my father utterly despised. I have always loved landscape painting, and assembled perhaps Europe's largest collection of nineteenth century American, so-called Luminist paintings, as well as very fine Impressionist paintings by Monet, Renoir, van Gogh and Manet among others. My first purchase of a twentieth century work of art was Nolde's watercolour *Young Couple* which is included in this exhibition. In rapid succession, works by other German Expressionists such as Schmidt-Rottluff, Kirchner, Marc and Macke started filling my private rooms. Through the work of Kandinsky, I developed an interest in Russian Avant-Garde—the Constructivists and Suprematists—and subsequently virtually all major movements and artists in twentieth century art: Cubism (Picasso and Braque), Surrealism (Ernst, Miró, and Dalí), Abstract Expressionism (Pollock and Gorky), Pop Art (Lichtenstein and Wesselmann) and Photo Realism (Estes and Bell). The most recent work in the collection is my portrait *Man in a Chair*, painted by Lucian Freud less than ten years ago. Now—about thirty years after my first purchase of a modern work of art—the Collection with its over 1460 works includes far more Modern paintings than Old Masters. Of these, only a few Expressionists and Impressionists have briefly been exhibited at the Villa Favorita. It is probably the desire of any collector to preserve, for posterity, the fruits of a lifetime of collecting and to wish to see the collection complete and intact. I created the Thyssen-Bornemisza Foundation in 1986, to provide a formal, legal, and administrative structure through which the Collection would be professionally cared for in the future. The Gallery of Villa Favorita provides a maximum exhibition space for 350 paintings and art objects. It has been my major concern during the past years to find the ways and means to create permanent exhibition space to show, if not the totality of the Collection, then at least the greater part. I believe that the masterpieces of world art are the artistic and cultural heritage of us all—an enduring testimony to mankind's history and progress. They should be accessible to as many people as possible. When the Kingdom of Spain offered me an entirely renovated palace across from the Prado in Madrid, as a ten-year home for over 750 of my Old and Modern Masters, I happily accepted this solution to the Villa Favorita's problem of space and exposure. In October 1992, after one of greatest moves of works of art of this century, the Museo Thyssen-Bornemisza was opened in the former Palacio Villahermosa. It was the first time I myself had the incredible experience of seeing the major part of my paintings hanging together. I must admit, I was impressed. Since then, to my personal satisfaction, more than three thousand people visit the museum daily, and I hope to find a solution with the Kingdom of Spain for the Museo Thyssen-Bornemisza to become a permanent home for the paintings currently on loan. Another, but smaller selection of about sixty Old Master paintings from my collection, are now exhibited at the renovated fourteenth-century Cloister of Pedralbes in Barcelona.

When all the Old Masters were taken off the walls, packed and shipped to Madrid, it was clear that we could and should do something completely new with the space. There were still nearly seven hundred paintings in the collection from which a new permanent installation of works was selected. After a major transformation, the Villa Favorita now opens its doors again. Inside the gallery, everything has changed through the biggest and most thorough of renovations since it was built. For a year and a half, the gallery and curatorial staff have worked on the transformation of the gallery to a bright, light, new, and fresh display of European and American nineteenth- and twentieth-century paintings and watercolours which were never previously on view. With this new installation, the Villa Favorita and the Collection it houses have assumed a new image and look ahead to the future.

Hans Heinrich Thyssen-Bornemisza

Europe and America
19th and 20th Century
Paintings and Watercolours
from the Thyssen-Bornemisza Collection

19th Century American Paintings
A European taste for American nineteenth-century painting took long to develop and refine. When nineteenth century American artists made the grand tour of Europe, often staying for years in Paris, Munich, London or Rome,
they sold very few works to private and public collections
on this continent. Baron Thyssen-Bornemisza started acquiring ninenteeth century American paintings in the late
1970s. Today, his is the foremost European collection of
this period. The Thyssen-Bornemisza Collection includes
important works from 1835 to 1900 by the major exponents
of the first indigenous American schools of painting; the
Hudson River and Luminist Schools; as well as the leading
masters of American Impressionism and Western painting. From 1815, America went through a period of prosperity and optimism. Industrialisation was growing, urbanisation was rampant, cultivation of new lands was rapidly
encroaching on the wilderness and railroads were carrying
civilisation across the continent. There was a sense among
Americans that land, space, resources and possibilities in
their country were inexhaustible, and that they were privileged because America exemplified the innocence and
abundance of Paradise. In this context, landscape painting
became the genre in which American ideals and national
pride found full expression. In landscape, artists could
trace their natural environment back to the Garden of
Eden, and to the beginning of time. The Hudson River
School, which took its name from the New York river
where the artists painted, is known to have been the first
landscape painting movement to achieve wide popularity
in America. It spanned three generations of American
painters. The first generation of the school were those
born, like the founder of the movement Thomas Cole,
around 1800 (Cat. No. 8). A second generation which included Frederic E. Church (Cat. No. 7), Jasper F. Cropsey (Cat. Nos. 10, 11), William Sonntag (Cat. No. 43), and
Thomas Worthington Whittredge (Cat. Nos. 47-50), was
born around 1820-30. Samuel Coleman (Cat. No. 9), and
John F. Kensett (Cat. Nos. 31, 32), belonged to the third
generation. Characteristically, all these artists painted
outdoors in the vicinity of New York and the East Coast.
They expressed in their paintings a pervading faith in God
and worship of nature which was, at that time, in perfect
concordance with public sentiment. The Hudson River

School paintings became popular because they were easily understandable by all, regardless of cultural background. Their compositions are based on a structural scheme derived from the French seventeenth-century painter Claude Lorrain. The Claudian landscape formula prescribes an orderly and harmonious division of the pictorial surface into receding planes. Man is reduced to the scale of a minute presence in the grand scheme of God's creation. The Hudson River School and Luminist landscapes represented in the Thyssen-Bornemisza Collection with a series of very fine compositions radiate that beauty, silence and total peace which in the nineteenth century was seen as proof of God's presence.

Luminism flourished from 1850-75. It was not an organised movement, nor different in outlook or approach from the Hudson River School. Many painters here on view belonged to the Hudson River School and painted compositions that can also be called Luminist. In Luminist paintings, the brushstroke is imperceptible—erasing signs of the ego and personality of the artist. The Spirit of God pervades the landscape manifested as the quality of glowing light transfusing the composition. In Luminist paintings, light is traditionally characterised as "crystalline," meaning that it is sharper and brighter, cleaner and purer than physical light. The space is carefully ordered and movement and time are ultimately suspended. These qualities find their purest expression in the compositions by Martin J. Heade, the Luminist painter par excellence. In this exhibition, works by him such as *The Marshes at Rhode Island*, 1866 (Cat. No. 23), and *Jersey Marshes*, 1874 (Cat. No. 24), exemplify the stylistic characteristics of Luminism. Other artists, among them Alfred T. Bricher (Cat. Nos. 5, 6), William Trost Richards (Cat. No. 39), Sanford R. Gifford (Cat. Nos. 16, 17) and David Johnson (Cat. No. 28) provide additional examples of the variation and consistency of the Luminist mode.

As America, late in the nineteenth century, was transforming more and more wilderness into civilised land and sprawling towns, an awareness of the inevitable destruction of the pristine and sublime was pervading the representation of landscape with a note of nostalgia. It became an urgent matter to record a treasure about to disappear. America's Western frontiers, the home of the Indians, was the last to succumb to civilisation. The West as a romantic subject, a genre, was first depicted in a naive, if not a primitive manner by admirers of the Indians such as Charles Marion Russell (Cat. No. 42). The subject was gradually taken up and made more elegant by sophisticated painters, foremost among them Albert Bierstadt (Cat. Nos. 2-4), who exploited the grandeur of the West and, for a long time, dictated a veritable fashion in American landscape. The artists, who went West accompanying exploratory missions, recorded the topographical look of a place, the appearance of its inhabitants, and the daredevil trappers, settlers and scouts who were the first to venture into these unknown and often dangerous territories. "Going West" was vividly described in a voluminous literature of travel diaries, accounts and expeditionary reports. Life among the Indians is represented in this exhibition with works by artists such as Oscar Berninghaus (Cat. No. 1), Henry F. Farny (Cat. Nos. 13-15), William R. Leigh (Cat. No. 34), and Frederic Remington (Cat. No. 38), who admired the traditions and cultural background of America's native inhabitants.

The end of the Civil War in 1865 brought with it the gradual establishment of a homogeneous American cultural identity. Towards the end of the nineteenth century pictorial fashions changed. From around 1880, a group of American artists—principally Theodore Robinson (Cat. Nos. 40, 41)—settled in Claude Monet's home town of Giverny, France, in order to learn Impressionism through direct contact with the great master. These artists brought Impressionism to America where it became the dominant mode for around twenty-five years. The American Impressionists are represented by the leading painters of the movement which, besides Robinson, include Childe Hassam (Cat. No. 19), John Twachtman (Cat. No. 45), and J. Alden Weir (Cat. No. 46). They adopted the idiom in the United States and gave it a specific American flavour. Impressionism, as a movement, prevailed until the 1913 New York Armory Show introduced the latest trends in European paintings which, together with American painting of the twentieth century, will be further discussed.

20th Century European and American Paintings and Watercolours

From the beginning of this century to the present, the speed with which Modern painting on both sides of the Atlantic changed styles is remarkable. To summarize the complex thoughts behind the many stylistic manifestations of twentieth-century art must regrettably lead to simplification. The early part of the twentieth century saw the flourishing of different trends that would simultaneously lead towards Abstraction, while realist art never ceased to transform itself along its own path of evolution. Within the first decade, two main trends were established which appear in painting thereafter: Expressionism, which explored feelings, emotions, the subjective and the self (Edvard Munch: "I paint what I saw, not what I see"), and Cubism, which together with Suprematism, Constructivism and De Stijl represented the objective, the analytical, the intellectual and the mind (Picasso: "I paint forms as I think them, not as I see them"). Both Expressionism and Cubism were manifested in figurative and non-figurative painting. They both included some of the earliest formulations of Abstraction which has become a basic component of twentieth-century art. They represent the duality of the human emotional and intellectual make-up. In this exhibition, that covers art of the old and the new continent, we chose to organise the presentation along these two main axes, and to exemplify the evolution of Expressionist and Cubist-Constructivist concepts on both sides of the Atlantic, as opposed to dividing art of our century into that of European and American paintings. The ideas behind a revolutionary transformation of painting which occured when Expressionism and Cubism were born at the beginning of this century, were developed and propagated in Europe, and later taken up in America. Gradually the creative power centre shifted and, after World War II, America took over the leadership of artistic expression. In the Thyssen-Bornemisza Collection, this relationship is reflected through the proportionately larger number of European paintings documenting the early twentieth century stylistic diversity, but gives way to a majority of American paintings from the 1940s until the present day.

In the winter of 1906-07, Picasso experimented with the construction of form and space when conventional perspective was relinquished. With its angular forms and expressively contorted anatomy inspired by Cézanne's Bathers and primitive African sculptures, Picasso's *Demoiselles D'Avignon* of 1907 (Museum of Modern Art, New York), became a startling and inspiring novelty. He subsequently created a series of paintings reduced to "cubes," to "bizarreries cubiques." The term Cubism was coined and designated in 1910 as an active Parisian movement. In Cubist paintings, the artist shows a natural object from different angles simultaneously; the object is static while the painter moves around it, thus reconstructing different fragments of the object. In Cubist paintings forms are only suggested. The distinction between the object and space in which it is placed is blurred. The usual relation between perception and concept is reversed, and forces the spectator to think in order to see. Early Cubist compositions are characterised by a reduced palette in sober colours of grey, brown, ochre, black and olive green. These limited hues and the fragmentation of the object became the "recipe" for a Cubist technique which was immediately adopted by progressive artists in France, Russia, Italy, Germany, England, Holland and America as evidenced here. In Cubist works, the natural object is always present. The abstract potential of Cubism is implied in its conceptual premises and is soon thereafter developed into its own mode. Although, in this exhibition, there are no examples of Picasso's works, the influence of his invention is amply documented in European and American Cubist works by Alexandra Exter, David Kakabadzé, Vladimir Lebedev, Fernand Léger, John Marin, André Masson, Marie Vassilieff and Max Weber. Known to have experimented with combinations of Cubism and Futurism are the Russian Avant-Garde artists of which the Thyssen-Bornemisza Collection has a rich selection. Works such as Olga Rozanova's *Urban Landscape*, 1912 (Cat. No. 134), where light bounces off an abstracted version of a city structure and gives an impression of speed and movement, exemplify

Russian Cubo-Futurism. Another variant of Cubism and Futurism is Vorticism, established in England in 1915. Visually, it is substantially different from its French and Italian origins, and from its Russian Cubo-Futurist counterpart. With an almost romantic attitude to the machine, which during the 1920s and 30s came to typify progress, technology and a certain optimistic faith in prosperity, Vorticism idealises industry, and man as a heroic worker. This attitude to industry was widespread in European and American painting of the early twentieth century. Vorticism was practiced as a clean, systematic, Cubist style of surface patterning, as in William P. Robert's depiction of London's busy docklands *Dock Gates*, 1920 (Cat. No. 132), where the crowded pictorial representation centres on an incessant movement of heavy industrial equipment and workers. A similar view of the worker and his friend, the machine, permeates the creative output of Fernand Léger who, with Picasso and Braque, is considered one of the three leading Cubists. While Léger used the Cubist technique, he worked with strong colours, and preferred the curving planes of the tube to the flat and angular plane of the box; he was, therefore, called a "tubist." For Léger, the human figure was an object, like a pot or a pan, devoid of sentimental associations, as in *Man and Woman*, 1921 (Cat. No. 100). Léger was in America several times and lived in New York during World War II. His influence on American painting is considerable, and he was almost better known and appreciated there than in his home country. On the other side of the Atlantic, Cubism took on distinct American features. Max Weber was among the first American painters to transform New York's skyscraper architecture into a dynamic Cubist panorama, *New York*, 1913 (Cat. No. 149). A rigid, slick and cool variant of Cubism called Precisionism tended to glorify industrialisation and urbanisation. Particularly suited for the architectural representation of factories and industrial buildings, Precisionism was propagated by Charles Demuth and Charles Sheeler, as exemplified by Demuth's *Church in Provincetown No. 2*, 1919 (Cat. No. 69), and Sheeler's *Ore into Iron*, 1953 (Cat. No. 142). A loose and more undogmatic, decorative type of Cubism is represented in the cityscapes and coastal scenes of John Marin (Cat Nos. 108, 109). In this moderate form, Cubism became the predominant "modern" style in America during the 1930s. Most artists mentioned above had studied Cubism in Paris, and therefore brought back the formal and structural recipe which they elaborated in a more figurative and moderately abstracted way. While Cubism leads towards Abstraction, its basis has always been the object. Constructivist concepts originating in the Suprematism of the Russian Avant-Garde, however, discarded representation of the seen and known, and produced compositions which are purely abstract. Non-objective art entails the invention of forms which have no relation to objective nature at all and are therefore given this title. Abstract may denote non-objective, but it also refers to non-realistic paintings in which references to nature are either remote or oblique. Within a year of 1910, a number of artists in several different places gradually came to discover design divorced from representation and its limitless potential. The paintings shown by Kazimir Malevich in the St. Petersburg "Last Futurist Exhibition. 0.10" of 1915, consisted of painted geometrical elements such as squares and rectangles in black and white. Malevich had reached what, in his own words, symbolises "the supremacy of feeling in creative art." He proclaimed the square the most fundamental of artistic elements where "all references to ordinary objective life have been left behind and nothing is real except feeling…the feeling of non-objectivity." The Thyssen-Bornemisza Collection includes an important untitled Suprematist composition by Malevich from 1919 (Cat. No. 103), and Ilia Chashnik's *Suprematist Relief No.II*, c. 1926 (Cat. No. 63), which resembles an architectural model of a futurist city. The artist's work and theories were immensely influential on Russian Avant-Garde painters, but by 1922 Malevich announced that Suprematism was finished, exhausted, and he returned to figurative art. Malevich remained a devout Christian and his theories reflected a mystic spirituality, which was, unfortunately, not easily accessible to the masses. From the mid-20s, the justification of Soviet art was to be of social and utilitarian function. Before Socialist Realism was imposed as the government dictated style in 1932, Constructivism—while developing ideas from Suprematism—proposed to convert all aspects of design, architecture, applied arts, theatre, cinema and typography into an aesthetic-functional ingredient of modern life. The word Construction was used for the first time by Vladimir Tatlin in the title *Relief Constructions* of 1913-14. Constructivist artists represented in this exhibition include Varvara Stepanova (Cat. No. 145) and Paul Mansouroff (Cat Nos. 104, 105).

Elsewhere in Europe, painters exploring geometric nonfiguration in few bright primary colours gathered around the Dutch art group De Stijl. This movement took its name from the monthly publication of Theo van Doesburg (in print 1917-32), which exercised a tremendous impact on European art and design simultaneously with Russian Constructivists. While the artists of De Stijl were not concerned with social messages or reforms as were the Russian Constructivists, they were attempting to heighten the aesthetic beauty and quality of both the functional and utilitarian. The best-known artists of De Stijl were Piet Mondrian and Theo van Doesburg. Mondrian had been in Paris practising Cubism from 1911-14, and through his studies he concluded that Cubism did not advance enough towards the most radical reduction of objects arranged in orderly, systematic planes. Mondrian continued to completely flatten planes in his own compositions. In his paintings, vertical and horisontal lines at right angle intersections enclose fields of red, yellow and blue, or white and give the impression of a total departure from natural appearances. Through van Doesburg's Bauhaus courses from 1921-23, the ideas of De Stijl were disseminated amongst a large group of art students, including Karl Peter Röhl, whose *Schwarz-Blue (Grosses Quadrat)* (Cat. No. 133) was illustrated in issue no. 12 of *De Stijl*, 1922. Other De Stijl associates represented in this exhibition include Walter Dexel (Cat. No. 72) and Cesar Domela. *Composition No. 5 M, Lozange*, painted by Domela in 1926 (Cat. No. 73), has, like similar works by Mondrian, no centre and no focus. The tension is evenly distributed across the entire surface, and the composition is totally non-objective and, therefore, purified of all personal sentiment.

Foremost among the German Bauhaus artists represented in this exhibition is the Swiss Johannes Itten. The Bauhaus School was one of the most influential and exciting experiments in art and design education ever, due primarily to the strength of its teachers. Itten was one of the first artists engaged by Walter Gropius—the founder of the Bauhaus—and it was he who created the basic course required of all students upon entering the school. This course became a lasting and influential contribution to modern art educational theory. It brought tremendous stimulus to participating students, such as Röhl. The idea of an art school covering all aspects of artistic expression and craftsmanship had several points in common with the arts and crafts studios designed by the reorganisers of the Post-Revolutionary Soviet art educational services. After Itten left the Bauhaus in 1923, he remained an art teacher in Berlin and Zürich where he settled in 1938. Essential pictorial problems such as the nature of light were the theme of some important mature works executed in Zürich towards the end of Itten's life; *Gütiges Licht*, 1963 (Cat. No. 93), being one of them.

The tendencies described above belong to that category of painting which strives for the impersonal, logical and unemotional represented by clarity and precision. On the other hand, the twentieth century, more than any other time in the history of mankind, has been the century of the "ego", with an immense emphasis on the individual's own, personal inner stirrings and need for self-fulfillment. Those tendencies are here represented by Edvard Munch, whose powerful, emotional works of the 1890s, here represented by *Das kranke Mädchen* (Cat. No. 114), and *Begegnung im Weltall* (Cat. No. 115), heavily influenced German Expressionism. The term "expressionist" had already been used in 1911 to describe all modern painting, but soon it came to mean primarily German art. Expressionism releases moods, feelings and emotions through exuberant colour. No attention is paid to the "real" colour of an object and gestural brushwork discards "correct" line. This movement originated with the group Die Brücke which, in 1905, was formed in Dresden by four artists. Among them was Karl Schmidt-Rottluff whose watercolour *Dorf Dan-*

gast, 1909 (Cat. No. 137), represents the North Sea region around Oldenburg which became one of the favourite summer resorts of the Brücke artists. Emil Nolde, who joined the group a year later and ranks as one of Germany's most important Expressionists, made these Northern coastal areas his summer and later permanent residence. Nolde's flowers, figures and landscapes, five of which are on view, glow with intense, burning colours (Cat. Nos. 117-121). Expressionism, as it was practised by the Brücke artists can be called Germany's first modern movement. By 1911 all the members of the group had moved to Berlin, and by 1913 the group was dissolved when the individual artists pursued their separate ways. The history of Expressionism includes Wassily Kandinsky's investigations of the expressive power of pure colour, and their ability to exalt—like music—such qualities as moods and feelings. Kandinsky's experiments with abstraction in Munich during the years 1910-14 were painted "rather subconsciously in a state of strong inner tension." They had far-reaching impact on other local artists of the Expressionist mode. Kandinsky, Franz Marc, August Macke (Cat. No. 102), and Paul Klee are the principal painters of the informal Munich-based Blue Rider association (1910-14). Marc had chosen to use animals as symbols of spiritual purity and strength in his search for the psychic energy common to human and non-human consciousness. The Thyssen-Bornemisza Collection includes Marc's last watercolour *Pokal mit Fuchs und Rehbock*, 1915 (Cat. No. 107), executed just before his death in World War I. An American Expressionist searching for powerful imagery is Charles Burchfield. In his diaries, he kept note of his own intense perception of everyday events, and in his works he used a very personal form and colour selection, vesting images with symbolic references to the deeper and unseen, as exemplified in *Dream of a Storm at Dawn*, 1963-66 (Cat. No. 62). Burchfield stands as a singular example of the perpetuation of the Expressionist idea, which, during the late 1940s, American artists transformed into Abstract Expressionism.

Dada and Surrealism explore, like Expressionism, a representation of the personal, inner world of the artist while giving importance to the subconscious manifestation of the magical, mystical and irrational component of reality. The ideas and techniques of Dada and Surrealism foster a degree of abstraction in which the absurd and the disturbing are major ingredients. Dada invites chance and spontaneity as opposed to reflection and analysis. It provokes the mind and eye to see things in a new way. Through works by Marcel Duchamp and Francis Picabia (Cat. no. 125) exhibited at the 1913 New York Armory Show, Dada became a tremendous influence on modern American art. Picabia's representations of the machine have a sinister, threatening character, as in *Le Broyeur*, 1921-22 (Cat. No. 125). The earliest effect of Picabia and Duchamp on American art was through their friendship with Man Ray, here represented with *Trou de Serrure*, 1928 (Cat. No. 104), painted in Paris where the artist lived for many years. Man Ray's contribution to American Dada and Surrealism is considerable. Giorgio de Chirico's views of deserted city squares, pervaded by an eerie atmosphere of loneliness and unnatural silence—the metaphysical paintings (1915-19)—were important to the development of Surrealism and its later international success. De Chirico's mannequins represent the dehumanised aspect of modern man and provoke uneasiness, as in *L'Archeologo Solitario*, 1966 (Cat. No. 65). Max Ernst was one of the most remarkable Dada and Surrealist artists, and one of the masters of modern art. He believed in the symbolic image as the primary element in pictorial art. The mythical bird Loplop in *Loplop présente la Belle Saison*, c. 1930 (Cat. No. 79), became a metaphor of the painter himself in a large series of collages and paintings. Ernst explored alternatively representational and abstract expressions of the subconscious, the latter exemplified by *La Mer*, 1924 (Cat. No. 78) and *The Red Sun*, 1957 (Cat. No. 80). He invented, around 1925, the technique "frottage" (rubbing), and in 1942, when he resided in America, a drip-painting technique called Oscillation known to have been later adopted by Jackson Pollock. Both methods created suggestive images divorced from the brain's control, and were equivalent to the automatic writing prescribed by the Surrealist theory.

Abstract Expressionism evolved around 1946 with the famous drip paintings of Pollock which epitomize the culmination of the Expressionist emphasis on self and feeling, and the Surrealist subscription to automatism. Abstract Expressionism gave American art an international prominence for the first time. With this movement, American painting took over the leading position in twentieth century art. By the end of the 50s, Abstract Expressionism exhausted its broader appeal because of its self absorbing focus. In this Gallery, several of Pollock's important early Abstract Expressionist compositions (Cat. Nos. 126-128) are shown alongside works by artists whom he influenced, among them his own wife Lee Krasner (Cat. No. 96), Alfonso Ossorio (Cat. No. 122), and Richard Pousette-Dart (Cat. No. 130).

Though Abstract tendencies may have prevailed, Realism never vanished, particularly in America, where the Realist tradition was and still is very strong. Ordinary aspects of everyday reality have been the themes for the Ashcan School painters, established by Robert Henri (Cat. No. 88), and later Guy Pène du Bois (Cat. Nos. 74, 75), Edward Hopper (Cat. Nos. 90-92), Reginald Marsh (Cat. No. 111) and other artists with backgrounds in magazine illustration. The American Scene painters—among them Thomas Hart Benton (Cat. Nos. 55, 56) and Ben Shahn (Cat. No. 141)—concentrated on compositions which reflect social and political reality from the twenties through the forties. The popularity in America during the 1960s of Pop Art, and during the 1970s and 80s of Photo Realism—here represented by Charles Bell (Cat. No. 54), Richard Estes

(Cat. No. 81), and David Parrish (Cat. No. 123), is due to the use of bright and colourful commercial imagery. These styles are basically versions of American Scene painting combined with the imagery of industrial society first introduced by Léger's Cubist works. The immediate gratification of the recognisable brought tremendous popularity to these figurative styles and allowed for art to be easily accessible to all. The intellectual strain of interpreting obscure abstractions gave way to the easy delight of seeing colour and widely diffused imagery from daily life: commercials, TV, photography and cinema. Aspects of the American way of life appear in works such as Tom Wesselmann's *Bedroom Collage*, 1974 (Cat. No. 152), or with some tinge of irony and humour by immigrant artists such as Saül Steinberg (Cat. No. 144) and Richard Lindner. There is a strong element of social comment in *Out of Towners*, 1968 (Cat. No. 101), which reveals Lindner's German background and natural affinity with the Neue Sachlichkeit movement of the 1930's. Estes' *Hotel Lucerne*, 1976 (Cat. No. 81), closes the stylistic panorama of art represented in this exhibition with Photo Realism. Estes regarded his manner of painting as "an abstract way of seeing things without commentary and personal involvement." In his New York scenes, light is purer and brighter than physical light and therefore recalls that special quality of light of nineteenth century Luminist landscapes as discussed previously. In *Three Yamahas* by David Parrish, 1975 (Cat. No. 123), and *Thunder Smash* by Bell, 1977 (Cat. No. 54), the close-ups of cut off detail cram the picture space and create a high degree of visual complexity, which is typical of Photo Realism and part of its broad appeal.

The most recent painting in the Thyssen-Bornemisza Collection is the Baron's portrait *Man in a Chair*, painted less than ten years ago by one of the greatest living Realist painters, Lucian Freud (Cat. No. 84). The artist portrays the collector "caught in a moment between reflection and self-projection, his face naked as a hand." The paintings on view represent a small part of the over 1400 Old Masters and Modern paintings of the Thyssen-Bornemisza Collection. The twentieth-century paintings were almost all acquired by the Baron during the 1970s, whereas the nineteenth century American paintings were collected during the 1980s, with the most recent purchase being Twachtman's *Boats Moored on a Creek* (Cat. No. 45), bought in 1990. From the tranquility and God ordained world order represented in the nineteenth century American landscapes to the experimental art forms of the twentieth century, the extraordinary creative energy which pervades the last two centuries of painting are reflected in this selection of works from the Thyssen-Bornemisza Collection.

Elisabeth Storm Nagy

19th Century American Paintings
from the Thyssen-Bornemisza Collection

Cat. No. 1
Oscar Edmund Berninghaus
(or **Beringhaus**) (1874-1952)
Apache Braves, c. 1915
Watercolour on paper,
49.5 × 34.5 cm
Signed lower right:
"O.E. Berninghaus"
1982.23

Oscar Edmund Berninghaus first visited Taos, New Mexico, in 1899 as a young man working on sketches for railroad travel brochures. He became fascinated by the Pueblo Indians of Taos, a tribe that had managed to remain relatively untouched by the civilisation of the white man, and had preserved their culture and rituals. Berninghaus spent every summer painting—mainly Western subjects—in Taos from 1900 until 1925. Then he settled there permanently until his death. He first established a reputation as a painter of Western scenes in St. Louis, where he was born, but it was in New York in 1919 that he had his first one-man exhibition at the Babcock and Milch galleries. *Apache Braves* represents a small group of armed Indians, possibly from the area south of Taos, riding across the desert. The watercolour was painted close to the time Berninghaus became one of the founding members of the Taos Society of Artists (1915). Very little is known of Berninghaus' work after the late 1920s.

Cat. No. 2
Albert Bierstadt (1830-1902)
Sundown at Yosemite, c. 1863
Oil on canvas, 30.5 × 41 cm
Signed lower right: "ABierstadt"
[AB joined]
1980.9

Albert Bierstadt, who was German by birth, grew up in New Bedford, Massachusetts. In 1853, he went to study in Düsseldorf, then the leading European centre for young American artists. There he became friendly with American artists such as Thomas Worthington Whittredge (Cat. Nos. 47-50), Carl Wimar and Emanuel Leutze. After trips through Switzerland and Italy, Bierstadt returned to New Bedford in 1857. Numerous landscape sketches brought back from his European sojourn became the inspiration for some large-scale compositions. These works established his position as one of the most prominent and technically brilliant landscape painters.

During his most successful years — from the late 1850s through the 1870s — Bierstadt recorded the yet untouched natural wonders of the Rocky Mountains, Sierra Nevada Mountains, and Yosemite Valley on several exploratory trips. Back in the studio, he converted his sketches into grand panoramic views of the American West. When, in the late 1840s, gold was discovered in California large numbers of people crossed the great plains, investing their hopes for a brighter future in "the distant land of gold." The Yosemite Valley in California's Sierra Nevada Mountain range was first explored in 1855. Some eight years later, in 1863, Bierstadt went there during his second Western journey. The first reports on the spectacular scenery of the Yosemite Valley were enthusiastic descriptions of a place so overwhelmingly beautiful that it had to resemble the Garden of Eden, yet no artist had depicted this magical place. Sheltered

against time and intrusion by impenetrable granite walls, the waterfalls, lakes, forests, and wild life of Yosemite provided the artist with a wealth of visual impressions. Bierstadt camped for seven weeks in the Valley, making drawings and "plein-air" sketches to record the setting. In this little scene, Bierstadt captures the spectacular light effects of the glowing sun setting over the valley while cows water in a placid lake.

Cat. No. 3
Albert Bierstadt (1830-1902)
Mountain Scene (View in Yosemite Valley), c. 1865-70
Oil on canvas, 56 × 77.6 cm
Signed lower left: "ABierstadt"
[AB joined]
1980.13

It was customary for nineteenth century American artists such as Albert Bierstadt to collect sketches while travelling in Europe and Western America. Large compositions, often drawn from these sketches, were executed back in the studio. In this sense, Bierstadt was not concerned with topographical accuracy; he combined specifics with invention to create an imagined scene. Many landscapes such as *Mountain Scene* (also known as *View in Yosemite Valley*), are, as these titles indicate, impossible to identify; having elements that resemble views from the Bernese Alps in Switzerland, the Rocky Mountains, or the Sierra Nevada Mountains in the United States. Certain compositional elements were used again and again by Bierstadt, such as the group of detailed pine trees in the foreground, some healthy and green, others withering away and tilted in dramatic silhouettes against the mountains in the far distance. The snow white peaks catching the sunlight somewhere between mist and clouds in the background of this composition bring to mind elements used in landscapes from the Lauterbrunnen Valley in the Bernese Oberland—such as the dramatic Staubbach Falls and the peaks of the Silberhorn closing the valley in the distance of *Majesty of the Mountains* (Jon and Barbara Landau Collection, New York)—which were painted after Bierstadt's first trip to Switzerland in 1857.

Cat. No. 4
Albert Bierstadt (1830-1902)
The Falls of St. Anthony,
c. 1880-87
Oil on canvas, 97.3 × 153 cm
Signed lower left: "ABierstadt"
[AB joined]
1980.8

The Falls of St. Anthony on the upper stretches of the Mississippi River in Minnesota were discovered in 1680 by a Franciscan missionary, Father Hennepin, who had been taken captive by the Sioux Indians. By the time Albert Bierstadt visited Minnesota in the 1880s, the Falls had already been totally incorporated into the expanding city of Minneapolis. It is in fact an imagined, romantic and idealized view of the Falls Bierstadt presents in this composition. He exaggerated the true proportions of the Falls, stretching the cascades of falling water dramatically across the wide, panoramic scene. A dark pensive figure in the fore-

ground, seen from behind as in the tradition of Caspar David Friedrich's German Romantic paintings, stands out against the flowing water contrasting with the magnificent sunset. An Indian in a canoe at the edge of the Falls and two other Indians seated in the foreground, seem to be part of the landscape. It is possible that the scene represents Father Hennepin discovering the Falls and the three Indians are a reference to his Sioux captivity. Bierstadt took a great interest in portraying the wilderness of the West, since his first long cross-country voyage along the Overland Trail in 1859 as a member of the mapping expedition of Colonel Frederick Lander. Scenes of the West were among Bierstadt's early triumphs, as well as his late defeat; his great entry for the 1889 Paris Exposition Universelle *The Last of the Buffalo*, 1888 (Corcoran Gallery of Art, Washington, D.C.), painted shortly after *The Falls of St. Anthony*,

was considered outdated and rejected by the American Art Selection Committee. With the construction of the cross-country railroad, the famous sights of the idyllic American wilderness became more easily accessible from the 1880s onward and the novelty and mystery wore off. Consequently, Bierstadt's compositions grew out of fashion.

Cat. No. 5
Alfred Thompson Bricher
(1837-1908)
Hunter in the Meadows of Old Newburyport, Massachusetts,
c. 1873
Oil on canvas, 56 × 112 cm
Signed lower left: "AT Bricher"
[ATB joined]
1980.83

Alfred Thompson Bricher was only twenty-one years old when he set up his studio in his home town of Newburyport, Massachusetts. Bricher was a rather solitary man who preferred to be out in nature rather than working indoors. Although he painted for some years at the Studio Building in Boston (1861-63) and subsequently installed himself in New York in 1868, his love for the flat meadows of the Newburyport countryside is reflected repeatedly over the years, as in this composition. *Hunter in the Meadows of Old Newburyport, Massachusetts* is based on a watercolour of the same year in which Bricher won both admission to the American Water-Color Society in New York, and several complimentary reviews in the *New York Times*. As a painter, Bricher was a realist who did not allow his deep love for a particular place and scenery to become romantic or sentimental. With clarity and stillness—which is typical of the Luminist school of painting—this composition depicts a man hunting alone in the green on a quiet summer day. Bricher's human figure becomes part of nature like the trees, the water and the animals—no more important than any other living organism. This composition closely relates to an earlier painting *Cloudy Day, Rhode Island* of 1861 (Museum of Fine Art, Boston) by a contemporary in the Newburyport area, Martin Johnson Heade (Cat. Nos. 21-24).

Cat. No. **6**
Alfred Thompson Bricher
(1837-1908)
Low Tide at Yellow Gail Cove,
c. 1890-1900
Oil on canvas, 63.5 × 132.5 cm
Signed lower right:
"ATBricher" [ATB joined]
1980.76

Alfred Thompson Bricher is best known for his marine compositions—a subject he increasingly turned to over the years. He travelled frequently along the coast from Maine as far as Nova Scotia. A modest man and a quiet observer, Bricher was best at harmony with himself when out in nature, carefully depicting what he saw without trying to leave a trace of his own emotion or his own personality. In Luminist compositions, details are crisp, sharp and meticulous. Light is of almost metallic, "crystalline" clarity. Movement is frozen and time is suspended to convey a sense of divine perma-

nence. The resulting effect of "extreme" realism is somewhat comparable to Photo Realism of the 1970s. In this narrow, panoramic composition, the clouds are not moving, the distant ship is not sailing, the waves are not breaking, and the birds are suspended in mid-air. Only the eye of the viewer moves to follow the shimmer of light across the surface of the composition. The exact location of Yellow Gail Cove is not known but, often in Luminist paintings, time and place are immaterial.

Cat. No. 7
Frederic Edwin Church
(1826-1900)
Icebergs and Wreck in Sunset,
c. 1860
Oil on paperboard and canvas,
21 × 33.7 cm
1982.10

In the mid-nineteenth century, Americans were discovering that they were the priviliged inhabitants of a vast and wondrous land, varied and rich in resources and beauty. This growing sentiment of national pride promoted landscape painting to the dominant art genre. The works of Thomas Cole (Cat. no. 8), and his great pupil Frederic Edwin Church set the standard for American landscape painting—grand, fantastic panoramas suffused with light—reminding the viewer of the Garden of Eden and the omnipresence of God. To penetrate where no man had set foot and depict nature in all its splendour as God had created it

became the mission of American landscape artists. Church explored not only his native country but undertook travels to the mysterious and exotic regions of South and Latin America and the Arctic region of Northern Canada. His most successful paintings were South American landscapes, such as *Heart of the Andes* (Metropolitan Museum, New York), exhibited in 1859. In the summer of that same year, Church made a three-week voyage to Labrador to paint icebergs. He was fascinated with the icy scenery and the heroic tales of great explorers perishing in these deadly waters. During his trip he made several pencil and oil sketches and reworked the material over the next year in preparation for the great composition of 1861, *The Icebergs* (Dallas Museum of Art). The present small oil study, *Icebergs and Wreck in Sunset,* was one stage of the pictorial formulation of the final composition. The lonely wreck battered

against the rocky formations of the huge ice masses is a homage to Sir John Franklin who died in the Arctic in 1847. In the final composition, the wreck is reduced to a broken mast, a compelling sign of man's extreme fragility in the forces of nature.

Cat. No. 8
Thomas Cole (1801-1848)
View of the Arno, c. 1835-38
Oil on canvas, 81.5 × 130.3 cm
Signed right edge: "T.Cole"
1980.16

Thomas Cole emigrated from England to America at the age of nineteen. At this time, the greater part of America was unexplored. Every motif was new and fresh. Every spot was untouched and the wealth and variety of natural settings were immense. A profoundly religious man, Cole viewed the wilderness of the American landscape as a powerful manifestation of God's presence. He briefly trained at the Pennsylvania Academy of Fine Arts. In the summer of 1825 he discovered the scenery along the Hudson River and became the founder of the Hudson River School of painting. By 1826, Cole had become one of the most eminent American landscape painters, and was soon able to finance a Eu-

ropean tour. He stayed in Europe from 1829 to 1832, and nowhere was he happier than in Florence, Italy, where he spent twelve months. Cole loved the view down the River Arno with the cypress lined villas along the river. He made a total of six compositions closely resembling *View of the Arno*, during and after his European stay. This composition, of c. 1835-38, was probably commissioned by a Boston collector, as Italianate scenes were particularly favoured by Bostonians. For Cole himself, but also for other American travellers who could look back on idyllic days in Florence, the scene of picturesque boats carrying people from one side of the river to the villas on the other side in the sunset evoked delightful memories: "The Italy we dreamed of... of romance, poetry" as Cole expressed himself in an 1832 letter to the Philadelphia collector Robert Gilmor.

Cat. No. 9
Samuel Colman (1832-1920)
View on the Hudson, c. 1865-69
Oil on canvas, 38.3 × 76.2 cm
Signed lower left: "Sam' Colman"
1980.17

Samuel Colman—the son of a dealer in books and engravings—grew up in New York, surrounded by artists and writers. During the 1850s, the young artist is known to have shared a studio with Sanford R. Gifford (Cat. Nos. 16, 17) and Asher B. Durand and to have started a life-long friendship with George Inness (Cat. No. 27). Colman's versatility extended beyond any narrow classification, but his friendships tended towards artists of the Hudson River School of painting. A European pilgrimage was a necessary part of the education of nineteenth century American artists and generally left great impressions and memories from which they drew for the rest of their lives. Colman travelled to Europe several times, first in 1860-61, and again during the 1870s. He then took several excursions to North Africa, Western America, Mexico, and Canada. *View on the Hudson* was painted during the second part of the 1860s when Colman executed several important Hudson River Scenes, including his most famous work *Storm King on the Hudson* of 1866 (National Museum of American Art, Smithsonian Institution, Washington, D.C.). This composition is sharply focused on the stones and rocks bordering the river bank in the foreground and on the group of sailboats, motionless on the river, in the background.

Cat. No. **10**
Jasper Francis Cropsey
(1823-1900)
*Ideal Landscape: Homage
to Thomas Cole*, 1850
Oil on canvas, 20.5 × 30.7 cm
Signed with initials and dated
lower left:
"JFC 1850"
1981.47

Jasper Francis Cropsey showed
great talent for drawing as a young
boy. At the age of fourteen he was
apprenticed to the New York architect Joseph Trench, in whose offices he remained until 1842, the
year he discovered that painting,
not architecture was his true voca-
tion. A year after leaving Trench,
he exhibited his first landscape
painting at the National Academy
of Design, New York. During the
1840s, Cropsey made extensive
trips both abroad and at home in
search of education and stimula-
tion. Cropsey greatly admired the
older Thomas Cole (Cat. No. 8),

whom he considered "the first
American landscape painter of
eminence." Cropsey's great respect for Cole is acknowledged by
this painting. In 1848—the year
that Cole died—Cropsey was staying at Cole's former studio in
Rome. Immediately upon his return to America in 1849, he visited
Cole's widow and saw the artist's
Catskill studio which had remained untouched since his death.
After seeing both finished and unfinished paintings in his studio,
Cropsey painted this little oil
study in the tradition of Cole's last
religious compositions—"The Cross
and the World" series. Cropsey
hoped to achieve that religious
feeling which radiates from Cole's
landscapes. A distinct feature in
Cole's last paintings was a celestial
light in the shape of—or radiating
from—a cross. *Ideal Landscape:
Homage to Thomas Cole* represents the garden of Eden with two
tiny figures pointing to a heavenly,
cruciform light appearing over a

bridge in the distance. The fluffy
clusters of trees with thick vines
growing up the tree trunks are
typical of Cropsey's compositions.
During the 1850s, Cropsey turned
to a less solemn and more bucolic,
pastoral view of nature, as in *View
near Sherburne, Chenango County, New York* of 1853 (Cat. No. 11).

Cat. No. **11**
Jasper Francis Cropsey
(1823-1900)
View near Sherburne, Chenango County, New York, 1853
Oil on canvas, 61.5 × 105.2 cm
Signed and dated lower right:
"J.F. Cropsey/ 1853"
1980.18

Although Jasper Francis Cropsey resided in Rome—at Cole's former studio—for some time, and was very impressed with the beauty of Italy, it was especially Vermont, New York and New England that appealed to him. Cropsey passed through the Susquehanna Valley in New York State on his way to Niagara Falls in 1852. He found the gentle hills and the lush greens of the fields, meadows and trees very beautiful and decided to spend several days sketching in the valley. Cropsey found the cultivated, "domesticated" landscape, with neat houses, farms, mills, and people going about their chores more in-teresting than the unpopulated wilderness. He depicted life in the countryside with a festive, patriotic spirit. *View near Sherburne, Chenango County, New York* represents the idyllic side of rural life, where people are boating and having picnics on the river bank on a lazy summer day.

Cat. No. **12**
George Harvey Durrie
(1820-1863)
Autumn in New England,
Cider-Making, 1863
Oil on canvas, 66 × 92 cm
Signed and dated lower right:
"GH Durrie/1863"
1983.32

This charming harvest scene from New England is one of the last works painted before George Harvey Durrie's death. Durrie, who spent most of his life in and around New Haven, Connecticut, had originally trained as a coach and sign painter. Throughout his life, Durrie preferred genre pictures filled with details of rustic life such as clapboard houses, farm animals and toy-like peasant figures often arranged around a central tree. In the mid-1850s he introduced harvest scenes filled with a particular exuberance to his general repertoire of winter and genre scenes. *Autumn in New England, Cider-*

Making—the smaller of two scenes of an apple harvest and cider-making—depicts the landmark of West Rock, New Haven, as the background for such an idyllic landscape with the intense yellow and red colours so typical of the New England autumn.

Cat. No. **13**
Henry F. Farny (1847-1916)
New Territory, 1893
Gouache on paper mounted
on board, 24.8 × 40.4 cm
Signed and dated lower right:
"H.F. Farny. / 1893/ ⊙"
1980.72

Since the mid-1860s Henry F. Farny had worked primarily as an illustrator for magazines (*Harper's
Weekly*, *The Century Magazine*)
in Cincinnati, Ohio, where he
spent the greater part of his life,
but also in New York. It was not
until 1890 that he chose to become a
full-time painter. At the end of the
1870s, Farny travelled regularly to
Europe and studied painting in
Rome, Düsseldorf, Venice, and
Munich. During the 1880s the artist made several trips West collecting sketches, artifacts, and photographs which he used both in his
illustration work, and later in his
paintings. Farny established his
reputation as an illustrator and

painter of Western subjects during
this period, and continued to be regarded as one of the masters of the
genre. His interest in paintings,
representing the life and customs
of American Indians, coincided
with the severe curbing of their
territorial freedom. From the
early 1890s, Indians were confined
to reservations and were forced to
change their ancient traditions. In
this context, scenes of life among
the Indians were painted with a
sense of urgency, even nostalgia.
It was seen as important to record
in detail every aspect of the cultural heritage of these proud people.
New Territory depicts an Indian
family crossing the desert on foot
and on horseback in search of a
new home. Farny paints the endless expanse of uninhabited, dry,
and sparsely-grown flatlands which
lie behind them in the bright sunlight. He calls attention to the anxiety with which these four Indians
look into the unknown territory,
and the future which lies ahead.

Cat. No. **14**
Henry F. Farny (1847-1916)
Indian Head, 1908
Oil on academy board,
24.1 × 16.5 cm
Signed and dated lower right:
"Farny./1908/ ⊙"
1980.84

This portrait is presumed to represent Ogalalla Fire of the Sioux Indians, who often posed for Henry
Farny in his Cincinnati studio.
Farny was in close contact with the
Sioux since he first visited Fort
Yates, Dakota Territory, in 1881,
while Sitting Bull was confined
there. It was the Sioux who allo-
cated Farny the symbol of the dot
within a circle with which Farny
frequently signed his paintings, including *Indian Head*.

Cat. No. 15
Henry F. Farny (1847-1916)
A Moment of Suspense, 1911
Oil on canvas, 61.3 × 41 cm
Signed and dated lower right:
"H.F Farny 1911/ ☉"
1980.4

The narrative of *A Moment of Suspense*, a scene Henry F. Farny painted several times after 1899, betrays the artist's background as an illustrator and storyteller: The deadly wounded grizzly bear has fallen in the foreground of the painting facing the viewer. On a narrow path amid towering, snow-clad mountains, Indian hunters cautiously approach the bear from behind. They are not assured to what extent the powerful animal has been exhausted, and whether they are out of danger. The landscape might be the area near Bear's Tooth Mountain in the Northern Rockies, Montana, first visited by Farny in 1881.

Cat. No. **16**
Sanford Robinson Gifford
(1823-1880)
Manchester Beach, 1865
Oil on canvas, 28.3 × 48.5 cm
Signed with initials and dated
lower right:
"SRG Manchester Mass.
July 17, 1865"
1980.21

The great majority of nineteenth-century American landscape paintings include some expanse of water: rivers, lakes, ponds, waterfalls, and seascapes. The ocean has always exercised a contemplative influence on painters and has challenged artists to capture the effects of light, the ceaseless movement of waves and the brilliance of the water's reflections. Drawn by the magic of infinity that both sky and sea represent, East Coast landscape painters of the period travelled and worked extensively along the shores of Maine, Massachusetts, and Rhode Island. The painters of the Luminist school such as Fitz H. Lane, Martin J. Heade (Cat. Nos. 21-24), John F. Kensett (Cat. Nos. 31, 32) Alfred T. Bricher (Cat. Nos. 5, 6), William Trost Richards (Cat. No. 39), Thomas W. Whittredge (Cat. nos. 47-50) and Sanford R. Gifford concentrated on the beach theme and produced outstanding works, several of which are exhibited in these rooms. Gifford executed this small oil sketch on a tour of the New England coast in the summer of 1865. He did this in the company of his artist friends James A. Suydam and Whittredge, with whom Gifford had also visited Europe from 1855-57. Characteristically, Gifford's tonality is warmer and more golden than the usual silvery clarity of the other Luminist painters' landscapes.

Cat. No. **17**
Sanford Robinson Gifford
(1823-1880)
Stelvio Road by Lago di Como,
1868
Oil on canvas, 24.7 × 20.5 cm
Inscribed and dated lower centre:
"Stelvio Road Aug 6 1868 Como"
1980.66

Sanford Robinson Gifford returned to Europe for the second time in
1868-69. There, he produced some
delightful oil studies of Italian
landscapes. *Stelvio Road by Lago
di Como*, executed in August 1868,
is a view from Lake Como in
Northern Italy which Gifford
found to be the most beautiful of all
Italian lakes. The road along the
northern shore of the lake runs
through a succession of tunnels
carved into rock. From the rather
unusual viewpoint of the cool dark
interior of one such tunnel, Gifford
painted the brilliantly sunlit lake-
shore drive, and a view out over
the lake. The artist successfully

tried to convey, as he noted in his
journal, that these tunnels "were
delightfully cool, like wells, going
into them from the hot sun." Gifford's underlying pencil outline of
the composition is visible through
the thin paint layer of quick, loose,
earthen coloured brush strokes.
This small study was used about a
decade later for a larger composition *The Galleries of the Stelvio–
Lago di Como* (Munson-Williams-
Proctor Institute, Utica, New York).

Cat. No. 18
James McDougal Hart
(1828-1901)
Woodland Lake, 1859
Oil on canvas, 117 × 183 cm
Signed and dated lower left:
"James M. Hart. 1859."
1988.11

James McDougal Hart grew up in Albany, New York. After a stay in Düsseldorf from 1851-52, where he studied with the landscape painter Johann Wilhelm Schirmer, Hart returned to his home town before setting up his studio in New York in 1857. During the 1850s, Hart submitted several landscape compositions executed with meticulous detail to the exhibitions presented at the National Academy of Design in New York. This led to Hart being recognised both within the organisation and among art critics as an eminent landscape painter. He was elected member of the National Academy of Design in 1857, and Associate in 1859. That same year, he submitted *Woodland Lake* to the Academy's Thirty-Fourth Annual Exhibition; *Woodland Lake* has never been exhibited since then. In a review of the exhibition, the *Saturday Evening Post* art critic described the painting as admirable because of "the graceful luxuriance of the foreground vegetation, the varieties of the ferns and other plants of low growth. The gleams of light here and there through the interstices of the foliage, the truthful gradations of colour by which the different planes of distances are preserved, all indicate a keen observance and a faithful and patient study of nature..." This early morning view of a deer by a quiet woodland lake is a major work from the period when Hart derived his greatest inspiration from the scenery of the Adirondacks.

Cat. No. **19**
Childe Hassam (1859-1935)
*Wet Day, Columbus Avenue,
Boston,* c. 1885
Oil on canvas, 38.3 × 45.5 cm
Signed lower left:
"Childe Hassam"
1989.3

Childe Hassam was born in Dorchester, Massachusetts in 1859. In 1875, he learned wood engraving in Boston and soon became a successful illustrator for magazines such as *Harper's, Weekly, The Century Magazine,* and *Scribner's.* In 1883, he made enough money to take his first of two trips to Europe. Returning from this first voyage, he carried with him a large collection of watercolours. They were immediately praised and exhibited in Boston and soon brought him great success. The artist took up oil painting and, before he moved back to Paris (1886), Hassam spent his time depicting the Boston parks and streets around him.

Hassam lived on Columbus Avenue and, on rainy days, he enjoyed painting this broad and busy street. He loved the reflection of the wet pavements and the misty atmosphere which subdued the contours of buildings and figures as in *Wet Day, Columbus Avenue, Boston.* These wet-weather street scenes, called "rainscapes," were said to have been invented by Hassam. Characteristic of these Boston views are the widely used brown earth colours. The most famous of Hassam's rainscapes of this period is *Rainy Day, Columbus Avenue, Boston* of 1885 (Toledo Museum of Art, Ohio) which is also one of his first major oil compositions. It was only during Hassam's second three-year stay in Paris that he became a full-fledged Impressionist. When he returned to the States, in 1889, he continued to favour the urban environment as his motif. This time, however, his palette was brighter, his brushstrokes were thick and spontane-

ous, and his base was New York City. By the early 1900s, Hassam was considered with Theodore Robinson (Cat. Nos. 40, 41), John Twachtman (Cat. No. 45), and Julian Alden Weir (Cat. No. 46), one of the greatest American Impressionists. Of all his contemporaries, Hassam had the longest career— he actively painted for over fifty years. He also had the most original, innovative, and imaginative of developments in which he specialised in the changing aspects of New York, the "asphaltic Eldorado," with its hustle and bustle. Among his most famous Impressionist compositions is the "Flag Series" of 1916-19. He also painted landscapes, mainly from New England; the Island of Appledore off the coasts of New Hampshire and Maine; and the Hamptons, which became his annual summer residence in 1919. Hassam was among the founding members of the group Ten American Painters which held exhibitions annually from 1898 to 1919.

Cat. No. 20
Charles Webster Hawthorne
(1872-1930)
The Kimono Girl, c. 1898
Oil on canvas, 76.5 × 61 cm
Signed lower right:
"C. W. Hawthorne"
1989.18

The Impressionists "discovered" the Japanese print, and contributed to the creation of a fashion for Japanese decorative luxury objects such as lacquers, porcelain, kimonos, screens, ivories, fans and prints. In France, the Japanese vogue particularly manifested itself after the 1867 Exposition Universelle. The flat, asymmetrical image derived from Japanese prints became one of the most innovative features of Impressionist compositions. The use of a two-dimensional space and the depiction of Japanese artifacts adapted to Western taste, established a new and exotic, decorative invention. Hawthorne was a painter of por-traits and genre scenes. He attended classes at the Art Students League in New York, and in 1896 to 1897, he was a student at William Merritt Chase's summer school at Shinnecock, Long Island. He continued his studies in Holland in 1898, where he broadened his knowledge of the work of Frans Hals. Hawthorne was primarily a realist concentrating on the depiction of fishermen and their lifestyle. He did, however, like Chase, produce a small number of Impressionist decorative paintings using the Japanese kimono as the main feature: *The Blue Kimono*, c. 1898 (The Parrish Art Museum, Southampton, New York), *Pink Kimono*, c. 1910, (Alexander N. Tschernjawski Collection, New York), and the Thyssen-Bornemisza Collection's *The Kimono Girl*. Hawthorne opened the Cape Cod School of Art, Maine, in 1899, and successfully directed this institution until the end of his life.

Cat. No. **21**
Martin Johnson Heade
(1819-1904)
Two Hunters in a Landscape,
1862
Oil on canvas, 31.2 × 61 cm
Signed and dated lower right:
"M.J. Heade 62"
1982.24

Martin Johnson Heade is considered a major figure in the development of American painting and,
with Fitz H. Lane and John F.
Kensett (Cat. Nos. 31, 32), one of
the most important exponents of
American Luminism. Heade spent
the first years of his artistic career
painting portraits and genre
scenes; it is not until the mid-1850s
that he turned to landscape painting. By then, he had spent several
years studying in Italy, England
and France (1837-40). On returning to America, travel remained
one of his great passions. He undertook many painting expeditions
throughout his life. Today, he is

mostly known for his landscapes
and a series of highly original
views of hummingbirds and or-
chids in the tropical rainforests of
Brazil which he visited in 1863-64.
Two Hunters in a Landscape is an
important early Luminist work
painted along the Massachusetts
coast, where Heade sought inspiration during the early 1860s. A
hunter himself, Heade was at ease
with the rhythm and laws of nature, and preferred the cool, grey
days of autumn to spring and summer. As rain clouds roll in from the
sea and darken the coastal landscape, the two huntsmen and their
dogs on the look-out for ducks are
scanning the beach. This action
draws the eye of the viewer diagonally across the composition from
the far right to the far left. The
narrow horizontal format, the diagonal move across the composition, the sweeping curve of the
finely outlined beach in the distance, and the clarity of detail are
all typical of Luminist paintings.

Cat. No. **22**
Martin Johnson Heade
(1819-1904)
Sunset at Sea, c. 1861-65
Oil on canvas, 54 × 91.5 cm
Signed lower right: "M.J. Heade"
1979.45

After having moved to New York in 1859, Martin Johnson Heade often sketched along the Rhode Island and Massachussetts shores. *Sunset at Sea* is one of Heade's relatively few seascapes, and one of his rare twilight scenes. These types of scenes were introduced into American painting by Frederic E. Church (Cat. No. 7) in 1860. They created a veritable fashion for rather dramatic and gloomy sunsets projecting an eerie sensation of tension and dark power. Heade observes the different cloud formations over the burning horizon, and contrasts the colourful tranquil sky with the turbulence of waves crashing against the rocky shore. The long, thin, light-tinged clouds above the water are so often used by Heade that they are a distinct feature of the artist's work.

Cat. No. 23
Martin Johnson Heade
(1819-1904)
The Marshes at Rhode Island,
1866
Oil on canvas, 56 × 91.5 cm
Signed and dated lower left:
"MJ Heade 1866"
1987.24

Martin Johnson Heade's first depictions of coastal salt water
marshes date from 1862, but the
artist followed this theme for more
than three decades. Initially,
Heade concentrated on the area
around Newburyport, Massachusetts, and Rhode Island. In the
present composition, the artist depicts the process of salt hay har-
vesting, where the hay was cut and
stacked to dry in large cone-
shaped ricks. In this early marsh
composition, attention is focused
on the details of the foreground
with its estuary bordered by the
characteristic green marsh grass
and the hay cart parked near a simple bridge. In the background, the
sunset with its magnificent tinge,
illuminates the clouds from below
and behind. The pattern of haystacks in the middle distance becomes less conspicuous, whereas
in later compositions, such as *Jersey Marshes* of 1874 (Cat. No. 24),
the main feature of the artist's
very personal rendering of this
particular subject becomes the
elimination of all other detail except the meandering pattern of
haystacks receding into the distance. In *The Marshes at Rhode Island* the quality of the rosy light
that bounces off every soft con-
toured cloud formation as dusk set-
tles over the wide open landscape
is characteristic of Heade's finest
Luminist compositions.

Cat. No. 24
Martin Johnson Heade
(1819-1904)
Jersey Marshes, 1874
Oil on canvas, 38.5 × 76.6 cm
Signed and dated lower left:
"M.J. Heade 1874"
1979.34

From the early 1860s through the 1870s and during the later years of his career, Martin Johnson Heade painted a number of marsh pictures in Massachusetts, Rhode Island (Cat. No. 23), Connecticut, New Jersey, and Florida. These broad, sweeping views out over a flat and uninhabited landscape where land and sky meet somewhere in a misty and hazy distance were particularly appreciated by both art critics and the public. Heade loved the picturesque pattern of newly-harvested salt hay, neatly heaped into stacks along a river, zig-zagging its way through a vast expanse of humid marshlands. Here, Heade treats a sub-

ject which Monet was to take up later in his haystack series of 1891. Heade's manner of painting, however, is quite different from that of the Impressionists. Often in Heade's compositions, man is included as a modest and small-scale figure, going about some solitary task such as fishing or hunting. The viewer is always reminded that man is but a tiny element in the magnificence of God's creation.

Cat. No. 25
Winslow Homer (1836-1910)
Early Morning, Adirondacks,
1892
Watercolour on paper, 40 × 56 cm
Signed with initials and dated
lower left:
"Early Morning, Adirondacks.
W.H. 1892"
Inscribed lower right in the
artist's hand: "Fog lifting by the
Adirondacks / Very Fine ⊥"
1977.109

Winslow Homer, who was born in
Boston, must be considered one of
the most American of American
painters. He was one whose art
signalled a turn towards truly specific American pictorial motifs and
technique. Homer's talent as a
draughtsman assured him, at an
early age, employment as a free
lance illustrator—first in his native Boston, and in New York after
1859—for some of the new flourishing pictorial periodicals with richly
illustrated essays. Working for

Harper's Weekly and *Ballou's Pictorial Drawing-Room Companion*
proved to be great training in
quick observation, assured handling and placement of both figures
and details. To this was added
Homer's love for nature, and a remarkable sensitivity to colour,
which found greatest expression in
his watercolours. In the spring of
1874, Homer exhibited, for the
first time, ten watercolours at the
American Society of Painters in
Water Colors, in New York. From
the beginning, Homer's watercolours were ranked among the
greatest achievements of American art. The critic of the *New York
Tribune* (February 14, 1874)
praised Homer for his "individual
way of looking at nature... [and
noted that]... These... mere mem-
orandum blots and exclamation
points... are so pleasant to look at,
we are almost content not to ask
Mr. Homer for a finished piece."
The vigorous "unfinished" quality—innovative, provocative, and

refreshing—is strongly manifest
in *Early Morning, Adirondacks*.
From 1886 to 1900, Homer was a
frequent guest at the North Woods
Club in the Adirondacks–a private
hunting and fishing preserve–
where he could combine his passion for outdoor painting with fishing and hunting. A total of around
eighty-seven watercolours were
executed during his various so-
journs at the Club, and these are
among the masterworks of his career. There are two main catego-
ries of Adirondacks watercolours:
one devoted to the theme of fishing, which constitutes about one
third of his total output, and the
other to deer hunting with hounds.
The luminosity of colour and the
economy of precise details sometimes, as in *Early Morning, Adirondacks*, border on abstraction.
In this composition the artist tries
to capture the density of fog lifting
over a chilly lake one early morning as two anglers set out in their
boat for a day of fishing.

Cat. No. **26**
Winslow Homer (1836-1910)
Gallow's Island, Bermuda,
c. 1899-1901
Watercolour on paper,
34.5 × 52 cm
Signed lower left: "Homer"
1977.7

Florida, Cuba, and the Bahamas became Winslow Homer's winter retreats from the mid-1880s onward. He found everything about the subtropics fascinating and strange: the exotic flowers, birds, and animals, the people; their appearance, costumes. The bold colours in the bright sunlight brought tremendous vivacity to Homer's palette. He adjusted his technique to bring out the vibrating intensity of the colour by keeping colour combinations clear within a simple, but strong composition. In *Gallow's Island, Bermuda*, saturated ultramarine and Prussian blues, turquoise and bright green liquid strokes are laid down over loose graphite outlines, reflecting the transparency of the clean water and the brightness of the white sand of the curving bay. At low tide, Gallow's Island (now Gibbet's Island)—a former place for public executions—could be reached along a narrow causeway, depicted in this composition.

Cat. No. **27**
George Inness (1825-1894)
In the Berkshires, c. 1848-50
Oil on canvas, 61 × 56 cm
Initialled lower left: "G.I."
1980.22

George Inness was still a very young man when he painted *In the Berkshires*. His formal training as an artist was limited to a short apprenticeship as an engraver with a New York map-making firm, and instruction from the French immigrant painter Régis Gignoux. With that in mind, one has to admire the talented and confident treatment demonstrated in this woodland scene from the Berkshire Mountains of western Massachussetts. Although the New York critics praised the fine technical achievements of Inness' early landscapes—including the Berkshire scenes—exhibited at the National Academy of Design from 1844 onward, they also reproached the artist for looking too much at Old Masters. Inness' use of chiaroscuro and his palette of greens, browns and golden yellows did emulate Dutch seventeenth century landscape painting. The upright format was, nevertheless, that of his "modern" contemporaries Asher B. Durand and John F. Kensett (Cat. Nos. 31, 32). During the 1850s and later he made several extended journeys both to Italy and France, where he encountered the Barbizon painters. Inness is one of those American painters who always preferred the "civilised" landscape—which also refers to Italian views—to the desolate grandeur of the American Wild West.

Cat. No. 28
David Johnson (1827-1908)
*View on the Androscoggin River,
Maine*, 1869-70
Oil on canvas, 71 × 112 cm
Signed with initials and dated
lower centre: "DJ. 1869.70"
Inscribed on verso:
"View on the Androscoggin
River. Me-/Above Shelburne-/
David Johnson 1869"
1981.44

David Johnson was a native New
Yorker who never left America in
search of inspiration and tuition
abroad. Nature, particularly the
region around New York and New
Hampshire, was his teacher. In
the company of artist friends such
as Jasper F. Cropsey (Cat. Nos.
10, 11), John F. Kensett (Cat. Nos.
31, 32) and John W. Casilear, Johnson's technique improved. He
achieved early on in his life—
around 1851—a high level of professional skill, and maintained a
reputation as a figure of some importance in American landscape
painting for more than thirty
years. Johnson's style was crisp
and clear with faithful observation
of every aspect of the landscape.
For a period around 1869-70, when
*View on the Androscoggin River,
Maine*, was painted, Johnson was
close to the Luminist mode. The
composition is from Maine, north
of the small town of Shelburne,
New Hampshire, near the White
Mountains. This location was quite
popular among landscape artists as
an alternative to sketching trips
along the Hudson River. In the
present composition, the calm surface of the river reflects the sur-
rounding landscape and the distant
mountains bathed in sunlight. A
tiny rowboat with a man—identified as the artist's friend George
W. Westwood—is the only sign of
human presence.

Cat. No. **29**
Eastman Johnson (1824-1906)
The Maple Sugar Camp–Turning Off, c. 1865
Oil on panel, 25.6 × 57.4 cm
Signed with initials lower right: "E.J."
Inscribed on verso: "The Maple Sugar Camp/North Fayette/Maine Turning Off/The hilarious occasion/Maple Sugar making" 1981.51

This unusual genre scene is inscribed by the artist on the reverse and refers to one of the most joyful rustic festivals in the Maine woods, in which the sap of large maple trees is tapped and boiled in a sugaring process. This procedure was carried out by large teams of people setting up camp in the forest while the sap was collected and treated. In the years 1861-65, Eastman Johnson followed the workers in his own mobile studio, from where he executed vivid sketches of all facets of the intriguing method from beginning to end: the "turning off" of the big cauldrons and the celebration at the completion of the hard work is represented in this oil sketch. A total of forty studies and oil sketches of the "Maple Sugar Camp" series were known at the time of Johnson's death, revealing his ambition to document a folklorique tradition which was bound to disappear. Johnson, who was primarily a portraitist and genre painter, had studied the technique of Rembrandt and other Dutch Old Masters in Holland from 1851 to 1855. He remained heavily influenced by Rembrandt's palette and free application of paint which is well reflected in the series representing the Maple Sugar Camp.

Cat. No. 30
Eastman Johnson (1824-1906)
Girl at the Window, c. 1870
Oil on academy board,
67.3 × 55.9 cm
Signed with initials lower right:
"E.J."
1980.23

When Eastman Johnson married in 1869 he was forty-five years old. This change in his lifestyle led to an increasing interest in the theme of women in a domestic environment. In the 1870s, Johnson made several interiors of girls and women alone. *Girl at the Window* probably dates from the very beginning of this period. Out of a dark interior furnished with a "whatnot," where various pieces of decorative objects can vaguely be distinguished, an adolescent girl is gazing through a window at a mother with a baby sitting on the steps of a building across the street. Traditionally, the motif of a woman looking out of a window—which was widespread in nineteenth-century painting—has represented romantic yearning for peace, love, and motherhood.

Cat. No. 31
John Frederick Kensett
(1816-1872)
Landscape, 1851
Oil on canvas, 75.5 × 63.5 cm
Signed with initials and dated
lower right: "JFK 1851"
1985.23

John Frederick Kensett began his
life in the small, modest town of
Cheshire, Connecticut. He ended
it in New York in a position of power and respect as one of the foun-
ders and trustees of the Metropolitan Museum of Art. From the time
of his father's death, his early teen-
age years were marked by strug-
gle and hard work as an engraver
of business cards and door plates.
By the time he was twenty-four,
he already had more than ten years
of professional experience as an
engraver—enough to earn him a
living while travelling and studying painting in Europe from 1840-
47. When he returned to New
York after the seven year Europe-

an sojourn, he was an accomplished artist noticeably influenced by the compositions of the
French seventeenth-century painter Claude Lorrain, and the Barbizon school. Back home, he made
many sketching trips with his old
painter friends John W. Casilear,
Asher B. Durand and Jasper F.
Cropsey (Cat. Nos. 10, 11) in the
Adirondack and Catskill Mountains of New England. His scenes
of Lake George, the Hudson River
and the Newport coastal area belong to the finest of the American
Luminist tradition. In *Landscape*,
painted shortly after Kensett's return from Europe, the artist's
training in the technique and compositional arrangements of Lorrain is very striking. A huge tree
frames the foreground with an
abundance of foliage and shrub-
bery. It sets the eye wandering
gently to a softly lit middle ground,
and from there to a background of
distant mountains bathed in a gold-
en sunlight. The yellow light col-

ouring the clouds over the horizon,
and the clear blue sky are typical
traces of Claude Lorrain's formative influence on American painting. The predominance of earth
colours in the foreground reflect
the works of the French Barbizon
School.

Cat. No. 32
John Frederick Kensett
(1816-1872)
Trout Fisherman, 1852
Oil on canvas, 48.5 × 40.6 cm
Signed with initials and dated
lower centre:
"JF.K 52" (JF joined)
1980.52

Trout Fisherman was probably
painted on one of John Frederick
Kensett's trips to the Catskills
where the landscape, the good
company of close artist friends and
the agreeable pastime of fishing
provided subjects for fine paintings. In this composition, Kensett
reveals his affinities with Asher B.
Durand, using a vertical format
in which birch trees form an arch
over the sparkling water. The dark
brown and green palette, however, is that of the Barbizon
School. The river winds its way into the dark tunnel of the thick forest, leading the eye towards the in-
conspicuous trout fisherman. In

Kensett's paintings, the human
figure is often present but only as a
note of colour, affixed to the landscape with no attempt at individual
identity or likeness.

Cat. No. 33
Ernest Lawson (1873-1939)
Stream by the Farm, c. 1902
Oil on canvas, 50.8 × 61 cm
Signed lower left: "E. Lawson"
1979.72

Canadian born Ernest Lawson belonged to a younger generation of painters who studied with the leaders of the American Impressionist movement. Lawson trained at the Art Students League in New York in 1891 with John Twachtman (Cat. No. 45), and continued at Twachtman's Cos Cob summer school for painters in Connecticut. Lawson was a great admirer of Twachtman, and his paintings reveal how deeply he absorbed the teachings of the older Impressionist. Lawson later studied at the Académie Julian in Paris (1893). During this period he came under the influence of Alfred Sisley. The artist spent another two years in Paris from 1896-98 before returning to New York City

where, in 1908, he became one of the members of the "Ashcan School" or "The Eight"—a group of eight painters concentrating on the theme of contemporary urban life. Lawson introduced the theme of the urban landscape into the range of subjects treated by The Eight. He enjoyed particular popularity during the middle of the decade following the establishment of this association. *Stream by the Farm* still falls into the group of landscapes most heavily influenced by Twachtman. It was executed around the time of Twachtman's death. Both artists had a preference for winter scenes but, in *Stream by the Farm*, the snow is not the clean fresh new snow silencing the environment—it is the messy melting end-of-season snow. The surface of Lawson's paintings form a particular pattern of sections such as the river, the road, the river bank, the sky, and the trees; all within which brushstrokes are applied in one direction

i.e. all horizontal, diagonal, or vertical. The texture is that of a thick crust of paint, also referred to as "crushed jewels of paint" which is unique to Lawson's compositions.

Cat. No. 34
William Robinson Leigh
(1866-1955)
Indian Herder, 1912
Tempera on board,
67.3 × 49.5 cm
Signed and dated lower left:
"W.R. Leigh/N.Y. 1912"
1981.45

After three years at the Maryland Institute of Baltimore, (1880-83), William Robinson Leigh left for Germany to study at the Munich Academy. He remained there for thirteen years. Leigh then spent the next ten years in New York working as an illustrator for magazines such as *Scribner's* and *Collier's*. In 1906, the Santa Fe Railroad gave him a free trip across the West in exchange for paintings illustrating the trip. His interest in the areas of Arizona and New Mexico as well as the Indians living in the Southwest of America—mainly the Navaho, Zuni and Hopi—led to annual painting trips to these areas, after which he returned to his New York studio with sketches. These were later applied to oil paintings, executed in the traditional, meticulous technique practised at the Munich Academy. Among the Navahos, women owned and tended sheep and goats and, since Leigh had an intimate knowledge of Navaho customs, the shepherdess represented in this composition is most probably of this tribe. The main emphasis of the composition is on the reclining, casual pose of the model in her poor, tattered garments, which recalls contemporary European depictions of gypsies or Neapolitan women. Leigh travelled twice to Africa in 1926 and 1928 as an artist working for the American Museum of Natural History, New York, and painted backgrounds for the Museum's African Hall. Leigh published two books on the subject of America's West: *Western Pony* (1935) and *Frontiers of Enchantment* (1938).

Cat. No. **35**
Charles Meurer (1865-1955)
Royal Flush, c. 1899
Oil on panel, 35.4 × 50.8 cm
1980.77

William Harnett, John F. Peto, John Haberle, Victor Dubreil, and Charles Meurer were a group of trompe-l'oeil painters who, during the last quarter of the nineteenth century, imitated US currency notes. The young Charles Meurer, a native of Cincinnati, Ohio, became so fascinated by the trompe-l'oeil still-life compositions of Harnett and Peto he saw at the 1886 Cincinnati Industrial Exposition, that he decided to make this category of painting his speciality. Meurer, who died in 1955, carried the Old Master tradition of trompe-l'oeil still-life forward into twentieth-century art, and almost lived long enough to see the use of currency as a subject matter in contemporary works by Andy Warhol, Larry Rivers, and Robert

Morris. *Royal Flush* was probably executed in 1899. A "Royal Flush" is the highest hand in poker, here depicted with an old and a new fifty dollar Confederate note from the Civil War. Such bills were no longer in circulation when Meurer painted *Royal Flush*, and he may have chosen to paint a non-circulating note in order to avoid being accused of counterfeiting. In a famous and amusing case, the US Treasury Department had confiscated Harnett's *Five Dollar Bill*, 1877 (Philadelphia Museum of Art, Pennsylvania), and a judge had to decide whether it was "a work of art or a counterfeit." Thereafter, artists were warned not to indulge in that type of painting. During the crisis of the 1890s, there was a proliferation of counterfeit money circulating. This forced the US Treasury Department to take such drastic precautions as the confiscation of paintings and prints.

Cat. No. **36**
Thomas Moran (1837-1926)
Windsor Castle, 1883
Oil on canvas, 93.5 × 152.8 cm
Signed and dated lower right :
"T. Moran 1883"
1981.22

Thomas Moran, born in England, made journeys back to his native country with his brother Edward—also a painter—in the 1860s to study and admire the works of J. M. W. Turner. Moran went back to England again in 1882, this time with his wife, the artist Mary Nimmo. Together, they toured the country's most famous castles and monuments. Moran returned to America with views of several English and Scottish castles. No other English site solicited such historic and romantic reverence as Windsor Castle, which had been painted by every major English artist, including Turner. The monument was on the itinerary of every American artist travelling through England. In *Windsor Castle*, Moran does not concentrate on the castle, but the vast park in which the castle is set. This painting depicts a small group of figures—possibly the artist's family—on the banks of a quiet river flowing through an idyllic landscape, with the barely visible outline of Windsor Castle in the distant haze. It is like a heavenly vision bathed in a golden light. Moran became famous in America for his views of Yellowstone and for supporting the establishment of Yellowstone as the first National Park in 1872.

Cat. No. **37**
William Sidney Mount
(1807-1869)
The Stone Bridge, 1843
Oil on academy board,
20.3 × 32.5 cm
Signed and dated lower
centre right:
"WM. S. Mount Oct 20, 1843"
1982.48

William Sidney Mount established
a reputation in the 1830s as a genre
painter; a reflection of his New
York apprenticeship with his elder
brother as a sign and ornament
painter. He was at ease with
cheerful everyday scenes, and
amused his critics and patrons
with clear narrative and luminous
painting. In France, Mount's
scenes were often made into lithographs where they were sought after as typical American scenes.
Largely self-taught, he felt a constant need to improve and perfect
his technique. In September 1843,
Mount visited Thomas Cole (Cat.

No. 8) at his home in the village of
Catskill. Together the two artists
sketched in the mountains, and
Mount took good note of Cole's
careful technique. After Catskill,
Mount went to Madison (now
Leeds), New York, and painted
The Stone Bridge—a local landmark in the Hudson Valley—on
the last day of his sketching trip.
This small vivacious sketch has all
the immediacy and charm which is
so difficult to convey in the "finished" large, meticulous studio
landscapes of the period.

Cat. No. 38
Frederic Remington (1861-1909)
The Parley (The Questionable Companionship), c. 1903
Oil on canvas, 69.8 × 102 cm
Signed lower left:
"Frederic Remington"
1981.7

Like Henry F. Farny (Cat. Nos. 13-15), Frederic Remington worked as an illustrator for magazines (*Harper's Weekly*, *Scribner's* and *Outing*). Since the first of many trips West to Montana in 1881, he had taken a particular interest in recording the costumes and customs of the Indians in their natural environment. Working as a sheep rancher in Kansas (1883-84), Remington acquired enough knowledge about the Indians to illustrate books on the West such as Theodore Roosevelt's *Ranch Life*, and *The Hunting Trail* (1888); Henry Wadsworth Longfellow's *The Song of Hiawatha* (1890); and Francis Parkman's *The Oregon Trail*. In 1889, it was Remington who won a silver medal at the Paris Exposition Universelle. The American selection committee rejected the large Western showpiece *The Last of the Buffalo*, 1888 (Corcoran Gallery of Art, Washington D.C.) by the established interpreter of the American West, Albert Bierstadt (Cat. Nos. 2-4), because his interpretation of life on the Western frontier was now considered too old-fashioned. In the 1880s and 1890s, life among the American Indians changed; mechanisation and urbanisation spread westward and overpowered them. In *The Parley*, the salute of the Indian seems to indicate his resignation and defeat by the white man and his powerful guns. The composition was painted in 1903 when Impressionism had changed the course of American painting. Between 1898 and 1919 the Impressionist group Ten American Painters which included some of Remington's friends, Childe Hassam (Cat. No. 19) and Julian Alden Weir (Cat. No. 46), dominated the artistic life of New York and Boston.

Cat. No. 39
William Trost Richards
(1833-1905)
*Seascape with Distant
Lighthouse, Atlantic City,
New Jersey*, 1873
Oil on canvas, 29.7 × 51 cm
Signed and dated lower left:
"Wm T. Richards, 1873"
1981.58

American landscape and marine
painter William Trost Richards began to concentrate on marine subjects and coastal views in 1867. Until 1874, Richards spent every summer sketching on the East Coast,
particularly the shores of Long
Island, Massachusetts, Rhode Island and New Jersey. Among his
friends were artists such as Frederic E. Church (Cat. No. 7), Samuel Colman (Cat. No. 9), Jasper
F. Cropsey (Cat. Nos. 10, 11), Sanford R. Gifford (Cat. Nos. 16, 17)
and John F. Kensett (Cat. Nos. 31,
32). In *Seascape with Distant
Lighthouse, Atlantic City, New*

Jersey, Richards depicts cool
waves rolling on a wide, flat beach
stretching far into the distance.
The lines of waves, horizon and
beach all lead to the distant lighthouse: the famous Absecon Light
in Atlantic City which still exists
today. The landmark was built in
1854, and was one of the most important lighthouses on the Eastern
Seaboard.

Cat. No. 40
Theodore Robinson (1852-1896)
On the Cliff, 1887
Oil on wood panel,
23.9 × 32.3 cm
Signed lower right:
"Th. Robinson"
Inscribed and dated lower left:
"Dieppe. June 25. 1887"
1979.17

Theodore Robinson is one of the finest and most important of the American Impressionists. He expanded upon an artistic education begun at the National Academy of Design and the Art Students League in New York, with studies in Paris from 1876-79. The artist returned to France again from 1884-93, spending most of his time there, but returning to New York for the winter months. Robinson probably first met Monet in 1887, the year he painted *On the Cliff* during a summer visit to Dieppe. In 1888, he moved to Monet's village of Giverny and formed a close and lasting friendship with the French Impressionist. He then became the leader of a group of American Impressionists in Giverny. Under the influence of Monet, Robinson rapidly mastered the Impressionist technique, as demonstrated in his works from the Giverny period (Cat. No. 41). The muted tonal values of the colours in *On the Cliff* do not yet belong to the bright colour range of the Impressionists, but the broad swirling brush strokes loosely covering the light priming of the wood panel are applied in a free and spontaneous manner. Form is defined by Robinson through colour rather than outline—as in Impressionist compositions. The young girl sewing on the cliff was Robinson's model Marie, whom he had met in 1886. Marie appears in a number of Robinson's most beautiful compositions throughout his Giverny period including his masterwork *La Débâcle*, 1892 (Scripps College, Claremont, California). From Robinson's diaries of the period, it appears that he was in love with Marie and had tried in vain to persuade her to marry him. The theme of the elusive woman is one that recurs in Robinson's work until the end of his career.

Cat. No. 41
Theodore Robinson (1852-1896)
In the Garden, c. 1891
Oil on canvas, 46 × 55.5 cm
Signed lower right:
"Th. Robinson."
Inscribed verso on the stretcher:
"Dans Le Jardin"
1981.59

From the moment Theodore Robinson settled in Giverny in 1888, and came in close contact with Monet, his paintings changed. *In the Garden*, painted a few years later, poignantly reflects this shift towards Impressionist technique of dabbing individual colour spots onto the canvas for recreating the shimmering and vibrating effect of dazzling sunlight. The blurred overall effect is, however, controlled by a firm underlying compositional grid. We know that Robinson often used photograhs for establishing the main structural elements of a composition: the placement of a central tree branching out diagonally towards the upper corners of the painting, and the woman standing very straight in the centre of this shallow space, crowded with undulating curving branches, were based on a photograph. The surface patterned with greenish, yellow, and blue-brown colour patches was finished outdoors. In Robinson's paintings, women are portrayed in worlds of their own: monumental, elusive, unavailable, absorbed in their thoughts and activity. The subject's gaze is always directed away from the viewer to emphasise the emotional distance which separates her from the painter and his audience.

Cat. No. 42
Charles Marion Russell
(1864-1926)
The Piegans Preparing to Steal Horses from the Crows, 1888
Oil on canvas, 57 × 94,5 cm
Signed and dated lower left:
"C. M. Russell/1888"
1982.38

The Western painting genre began as a description and recording of the American Indian culture in the last decades of the nineteenth century. Charles Marion Russell grew up in St. Louis, Missouri, but started working in 1880 as a cowboy on a farm in Montana. He worked near the territories of the Blackfoot, Piegan and Blood Indians along the Canadian border. Russell taught himself to paint and became one of the most prominent Western artists. He spent the winter of 1887-88 with the Blood Indians who had high regard for him and considered him a medicine man because of his talent for accu-rately depicting their surround-ings, dress, and accoutrements—pipes, feathers, bone ornaments and coup sticks. He was only twenty-four when he painted *The Piegans Preparing to Steal Horses from the Crows*—one of the fights between the Pigeans and their traditional enemies the Crows, which took place while Russell was staying with the Blood Indians. Hostility flared up between the Pigeans and the Crows in 1887 when the latter moved north across the Yellowstone River into Piegan territory. The Piegans retaliated with horse raids carried out in small bands as shown here in Russell's painting. At early dawn, horses are at rest before the battle while one man keeps watch. Four other Piegans sitting on a blanket are smoking long pipes, as was the custom before any serious activity. The scene is represented with charm and admiration for the life and customs of the native Americans.

Cat. No. 43
William Louis Sonntag
(1822-1900)
*Fishermen in the Adirondacks,
Hudson River*, c. 1860
Oil on canvas, 91.7 × 141.5 cm
Signed lower right:
"W.L. Sonntag"
1981.21

William Louis Sonntag grew up in Cincinnati, Ohio, and painted during the first part of his career primarily in his home state of Ohio and then in Kentucky and Virginia. In the 1850s, Sonntag made two long trips to Europe, staying in London, Paris, and Italy. He returned several times to Italy throughout his career. After he moved to New York in 1857, he concentrated on the scenery of New England. *Fishermen in the Adirondacks, Hudson River*, is an example of the large panoramas from the Hudson River area, which Sonntag refined in the 1860s. A low foreground richly painted in glowing, saturated colours sets off a mirror-like expanse of water flowing into the misty distance and framed by descending mountains and trees. In the "ideal" landscape, the human figure—in this case the two tiny fishermen in the foreground silhouetted against the immensity of the landscape—is there to emphasize the magnificence of nature and man's minute importance in the grandeur of God's creation. The axe-cut tree stump near the fishermen is a frequent landscape motif in nineteenth century American landscape painting. It is interpreted as a symbol of human progress encroaching on God's natural work. On the far shore, a primitive log cabin is almost lost in the wilderness—another reference to the feeling of limitless and untouched space which pervades American landscape painting of this period and contributed to the growing sense of national pride and identity among Americans.

Cat. No. 44
Alfred Wordsworth Thompson
(1840-1896)
The Garden at Monte Carlo,
c. 1876-77
Oil on canvas, 48.3 × 82 cm
Inscribed and signed lower left:
"Monte Carlo. Monaco/
Wordsworth Thompson NA"
1979.51

Alfred Wordsworth Thompson, originally from Boston, started out as an illustrator for newpapers and magazines. He lived and studied in France from 1861-68 at a time when artistic life in Paris was in a phase of great innovation. In Paris, he took lessons—like many French Impressionists-to-be—in the studios of Charles Gleyre, Emile Lambinet, the "orientaliste" painter Alberto Pasini, Aldolphus Nyon at the Ecole des Beaux Arts, and the famous animal sculptor Antoine Barye. The choice of subject matter and technical brilliance of Pasini made a lasting impression on the young American artist as did Mediterranean subjects. This influence was carried over into his production many years after his return to New York in 1868. *The Garden at Monte Carlo* was probably painted a decade after his return. By this point, artists in France—first the Realists, and then the Impressionists—had begun to place tremendous importance on the depiction of life in the city. Wordsworth Thompson, by natural inclination and training, excelled in urban scenes. *The Garden at Monte Carlo* belongs to the transitional phase between Realism and Impressionism. Wordsworth Thompson contrasted his careful and meticulous observation of details in the group of figures and plants in the foreground with the broad and loose contours of the park, mountains, and billowing clouds of the background.

Cat. No. 45
John Henry Twachtman
(1853-1902)
Boats Moored on a Creek, c. 1901
Oil on canvas, 72.5 × 50 cm
1990.8

John Henry Twachtman was one of the most original artists of the late nineteenth century. Twachtman was born in Cincinnati, Ohio, to German parents, and trained in Munich (1875-78), and Paris (1883-86) with some of the artists that were later to become the leaders of the American Impressionist movement. A few years after his return from Europe, he bought a large, beautiful property in Greenwich, Connecticut, where he lived from 1889 until his death in 1902. During his stay in France, Twachtman had become familiar with the works of the French Impressionists who later had their first epoch-breaking exhibition in New York in 1886. Twachtman only emerged as a true Impressionist after having moved

to his Greenwich estate. His preferred French Impressionist artist was Claude Monet, and there are obvious similarities between the two artists' works, particularly in the exploration of a single theme — "often a commonplace subject made beautiful by light" — as the critic of the *Art Amateur* observed in an article on French and American Impressionism (June 29, 1893, p. 4). In 1898 Twachtman helped found a group of Impressionists, the Ten American Painters, and was also a successful art teacher. 1890 to 1902 was a constant period of experimentation with Impressionist principles for him. The resulting works are considered not only to be a distinctive feature of American Impressionist painting, but also an outstanding contribution to American art. Although the majority of Twachtman's paintings from this period are views of his house and garden, some were landscape studies executed during trips around the United States,

and abroad. *Boats Moored on a Creek* is not from his Greenwich home, but as Twachtman hardly ever dated his works, it is often impossible to say with certainty when and where a painting was executed. In 1901 Twachtman spent the summer in France and painted in Normandy, near Honfleur. *Boats Moored on a Creek*, could possibly have been painted during this trip. The boats, the water and the wall of trees closing the background are only slightly differentiated in an overall tonality of warm, soft green, pastel colours.

Cat. No. **46**
Julian Alden Weir (1852-1919)
Silver Chalice with Roses, 1882
Oil on canvas, 31.5 × 23 cm
Inscribed, signed, and dated
on chalice:
"To Anna Dwight Baker from
J. Alden Weir/ May 18/1882 NY"
1980.54

This still-life composition of a Ba-
roque silver chalice and honey coloured roses in a bowl was painted
as a twentieth birthday present for
Julian Alden Weir's future bride
Anna Dwight Baker. Weir fell in
love with this young girl the instant she entered his New York
studio in early 1882. She had come
to him to take private painting lessons. He courted her gallantly
throughout the year and, by 1883,
they were married. In several letters written to Anna during the
spring of 1882, Weir described his
progress on her birthday painting
and his efforts to achieve a balance
between the fragile flowers whose
beauty reminded him of her, and
the hard, shiny surfaces of silver
and porcelain. Weir's finest paintings during the 1880s were still-
lifes, usually featuring roses. This
particular composition is painted
against a dark brown background,
as in Dutch seventeenth-century
paintings Weir had studied when
he made an extensive tour of
France, Holland, Belgium, and
Spain from 1873 to 1877. This journey was sponsored by Mrs. Brad-
ford Alden, whose name the artist
took in recognition of her support.
While a student at the Ecole des
Beaux Arts, Paris, under Jean-
Léon Gérôme in the mid-1870s,
Weir had seen Impressionist
paintings. He was initially critical
of their apparent lack of genuine
draughtsmanship, since he preferred the style of Jules Bastien-
Lepage. Returning from a second
trip to Europe in 1881, in the company of his great friend John
Twachtman, Weir soon settled in
New York. In 1882 Weir also became President of the Society of
American Artists which he had
helped found in 1877. He resigned
from this association in 1897.
Around 1890, Weir's own work began reflecting the Impressionist
aesthetic and, during the 1890s and
the first decade of the twentieth
century, he created some of the
finest examples of American Impressionist painting. Weir was
among the Ten American Painters
in 1898. Other leading members of
the group included John Twachtman (Cat. No. 45) and Childe Hassam (Cat. No. 19). In 1913, Weir
was represented with twenty-five
works in the New York Armory
Show. He continued exhibiting,
mainly with Ten American Painters, until shortly before his death.

Cat. No. **47**
Thomas Worthington
Whittredge (1820-1910)
Valley of the Ocale, 1865
Oil on paper mounted on board,
20.5 × 58.5 cm
Signed and dated on verso prior
to mounting: "W Whittredge
1865"
Inscribed lower right:
"Valley of the Ocale/[?]"
1983.33

Young Thomas Worthington Whittredge succeeded in becoming a
landscape painter in 1839—against
his father's will—after having
been a house- and portrait-painter
in his home town of Cincinnati,
Ohio. In 1846, he submitted a
painting to the National Academy
of Design in New York. Much to
his joy and surprise, he received
both recognition and praise from
the Academy's president Asher B.
Durand. This official recognition
made it possible for Whittredge, in
1849, to travel to Europe in search

of training. He remained there for
ten years, but always as an American at heart who loved his own
country. During this period, whittredge created warm and lasting
friendships with, among others,
the painters Albert Bierstadt
(Cat. Nos. 2-4) and Sanford R. Gifford (Cat. Nos. 16, 17). When he returned to New York in 1859, he
sought the company of the Hudson
River School of artists. He eventually became one of its leading members. In 1866 Whittredge made the
first of three journeys out West to
Colorado and New Mexico as a
member of an Indian peace-keep-
ing mission with Army General
John Pope. According to government documents, the mission left
Fort Leavenworth on June 1, 1866.
Whittredge travelled with the
group to Denver, Santa Fe, and
Albuquerque. He wound up at
Fort Riley, New Mexico in September of the same year. This narrow panoramic oil sketch shows
the barrenness of the open prairie.

It is a typical example of the many
nature sketches the artist brought
back from an expedition in to unknown territory. The date "1865"
which appears on the back of the
painting appears to be a later, er-
roneous, inscription.

Cat. No. 48
**Thomas Worthington
Whittredge** (1820-1910)
Autumn on the Hudson, c. 1875
Oil on canvas, 50.5 × 68 cm
Signed lower left:
"W. Whittredge"
1980.11

Autumn on the Hudson—probably painted in the vicinity of West
Point, New York—depicts the
pumpkin and corn harvests along
the wooded banks of the Hudson
River. The painting was executed
a decade after the Civil War, which
is noted as one of the most interesting and complex periods in American art. In this composition, Whittredge took to the broader, freer
treatment of paint which antici-
pates a shift in taste away from the
Hudson River style.

Cat. No. 49
Thomas Worthington
Whittredge (1820-1910)
A Catskill Brook, c. 1875
Oil on canvas, 77 × 113.7 cm
Signed lower right:
"W.Whittredge"
1987.27

Forest interiors—so called because the dense forest with its un-
dergrowth fills a solid, closed in
space—occupy a special place in
the oeuvre of Thomas Worthington Whittredge, a leading member
of the Hudson River School. When
A Catskill Brook was painted during the mid-1870s, Whittredge was
at the height of his artistic matu-
rity. *A Catskill Brook*, together
with a similar version, *Trout
Brook in the Catskills* (Corcoran
Art Gallery, Washington D.C.),
ranks as a masterpiece of the
1870s. During this period, however, the artist was the least productive in all his time. He served
as President of the National Aca-

demy of Design, New York, from
1874-77, and was consumed with
administrative work both at the
Academy and for the Philadelphia
Centennial Exposition. Following
the example of his friends Asher B.
Durand and John F. Kensett (Cat.
Nos. 31, 32), Whittredge had
painted forest interiors in the vertical format. The broad, wide view
straight up the silvery brook and
into the dense forest allowed Whittredge to close the visibility on the
sides and background of the composition. This elegant, horizontal
view of a forest stream lets patches
of bright sunlight penetrate the
luxuriant crowns of trees closing
high above the cool stream. The
viewer gets a distinct sensation of
the difference of temperature between the hot sun outside the forest and the fresh greens inside.
The beauty of the landscape in and
around the Catskill Mountains of
New York attracted many artists
since Thomas Cole (Cat. No. 8) settled there in 1836.

Cat. No. **50**
**Thomas Worthington
Whittredge** (1820-1910)
Seascape, c. 1883
Oil on canvas, 36 × 50.8 cm
Signed lower left:
"W. Whittredge"
1980.90

During the late 1870s and 1880s,
Thomas Worthington Whittredge
frequently travelled to New England during the summer. There
he painted scenes around Newport, Rhode Island, Cape Ann
near Gloucester, and Ipswich,
Massachusetts, as did a number of
Luminist artists represented in
these rooms: Alfred T. Bricher
(Cat. Nos. 5, 6), Martin J. Heade
(Cat. Nos. 21-24) and William
Trost Richards (Cat. No. 39).
Whittredge's seascapes of this period indicate affinities with Luminism in subject matter and, to
some extent, in the treatment of
light. *Seascape*, probably painted
at Cape Ann, is divided horizontally into three equal fields of sea,
sand, and sky—the classical Luminist way. It is, however, painted
with soft, pastel-like colours and
broad, free brush strokes. These
elements differed with the meticulous execution of Luminist compositions. The manner of painting
points towards the style of James
Whistler and the French Impressionists. Because of his open-mind-
edness towards new trends in
painting, Whittredge continued to
be a popular artist late into the
century.

Cat. No. **51**
Irving Ramsey Wiles (1861-1948)
Woman Reading on a Bench/
Sunshine and Shadow, c. 1895
Oil on panel, 35 × 43.7 cm
Signed lower left:
"Irving R. Wiles"
1979.23

Irving Ramsey Wiles was the son
and student of the landscape painter
Lemuel Maynard Wiles. The family moved to New York City in
1861, the year he was born. In 1879-
81 Wiles attended classes at the
Art Students League given by
William Merritt Chase. Wiles and
Chase—at that time the most significant art teacher in the United
States—formed a life-long friendship. Wiles spent the years 1882-84
in Paris studying at the Académie
Julian with Emil Auguste Carolus-
Duran. Back home, he made illustrations for the magazines *Scrib-*
ner's, Harper's Weekly and *The*
Century Magazine He also taught
at Chase's famous Long Island

school. In 1898 Wiles bought a
house at Peconic, Long Island, just
across the bay from Chase's Shinnecock house, and spent summers
painting there. *Woman Reading*
on a Bench/Sunshine and Shadow
combines the illustrator's mode of
precise expression, boldly outlining the foreground composition of
the woman reading on the bench,
with the impressionistic landscape, freely rendered of the flat
sunny Long Island meadows so often seen in the works of Wiles'
friend and mentor Chase. The
woman depicted is probably the
artist's wife, Mary Lee, sitting in
the garden of their Peconic home,
"The Moorings." Wiles travelled
several times with Chase to Europe during the first decade of the
twentieth century, and again in
1912. His personal style seemed to
have been firmly established by
then, appealing primarily to an
American audience. Wiles became
particularly famous in New York
as a fashionable portrait painter.

He reached the height of his popularity after his one-man show at
Knoedler & Co., New York, in
1910.

20th Century European and American
Paintings and Watercolours from the
Thyssen-Bornemisza Collection

Cat. No. **52**
Arman (Armand Fernandez)
(1928-)
Fiddle Marmalade, 1973
Silver and black paint on paper,
81.3 × 57.5 cm
Signed and dated lower centre:
"Arman 73"
1974.3

Arman's art is executed in the
Dada spirit of Marcel Duchamp
and Max Ernst (Cat. Nos. 78-80),
where the use of everyday objects—or fragments of them—as
provocative and puzzling artistic
statements shock our conventional
ideas of art and its aesthetic function. Even the name Arman is a
Dada absurdity, a misspelling of
his name in a catalogue of 1958—,
which he subsequently chose to
adopt as his artistic name. Following a brief period from 1949
through the early 1950s, during
which Arman painted as a Surrealist and became interested in abstraction, he developed his idea

of "repetition" or multiplication.
These ideas have since characterised the totality of his artistic output. Arman takes one type of common object and repeats it over and
over again in large compositions,
either painted, stamped, or as
sculpture embedded in plastic or
concrete. Arman became famous
in the 1960s and 1970s for his assemblages of rejects, garbage,
junk, spare-parts, and destroyed
and recomposed musical instruments. He says: "I did not discover
the principle of accumulation; it
discovered me. I am a witness of
my society. I have always been
much involved in the pseudobio-
logical cycle of production, con-
sumption and destruction." As a
child, Arman was taught to play
the cello; and thus musical instruments are often the subject of his
work. He has a strong affinity to
Japanese art, poetry and martial
arts. *Fiddle Marmalade* is a dynamic abstraction which combines
his interest in Oriental calligraphy

and musical instruments. In 1984,
Arman, who is French by birth
(but since 1963 spends most of his
time in New York), was commissioned to make a marble and gilded
brass sculpture for the Elysée Palace, Paris. With numerous museum shows and acquisitions all
over the world, Arman's art now—
shocking as it was at first—belongs to the establishment.

Cat. No. **53**
Milton Clark Avery (1885-1965)
Homework, 1946
Oil on canvas, 91.5 × 61 cm
Signed and dated lower centre:
"Milton Avery 1946"
1978.58

Milton Clark Avery was born in Sand Bank (later Altmar), New York. From 1895 to 1925, he lived in Connecticut where, beginning in 1905, he had his early training in lettering and life drawing. Avery attended various art schools for many years. Throughout his career he managed, nevertheless, to stay abreast of prevailing trends from Precisionism, American Cubism, Regionalism, and Social Realism, to Surrealism and Abstract Expressionism. The artist first exhibited in 1915 at the Wadsworth Athenaeum in Hartford, Connecticut, and, in 1918, he won the top honours in portrait and life-drawing classes at the School of Art Society in Hartford. When Avery moved to New York in 1925, he continued his studies at the Art Students League. In 1926, he married the free-lance illustrator, Sally Michel who, in 1932, bore him their only child. Avery was devoted to his family, and his daughter March became not only one of his favourite subjects, but also the lead motif of his first retrospective (1947, Durand-Ruel Galleries, New York). This exhibition was titled "My Daughter March" and *Homework* from 1946, was included as number 11. March was around fourteen years old when *Homework* was painted. As in most figure compositions from the 1940s, Avery left out, or barely sketched in facial features, thus reducing the figure seated in a colourful interior to large, flat, brightly coloured areas. Henri Matisse influenced not only Avery's happy choice of subject matter, but also the construction of the tilted interior with its bright blue chest of drawers, black floor boards, and large round-backed chair. An increasing simplification of motifs led Avery towards abstraction, although he never abandoned the object altogether. The intensity of colour and the simplicity of composition in Avery's work, particularly of the 1940s and 50s, appealed to younger American artists such as Mark Rothko and Robert Motherwell. Avery's talent and importance in twentieth century American painting were only recognized late in his career; he had his first one-man show at the age of fifty (Valentine Gallery, New York), and his first one-man museum show at fifty-nine (Phillips Memorial Gallery, Washington, D.C.). Avery's second and last retrospective exhibition was in 1960, at the Whitney Museum of American Art, New York.

Cat. No. **54**
Charles Bell (1935-)
Thunder Smash, 1977
Acrylic on canvas, 137.3 × 168 cm
1977.91

"In its obsession with Americana, Photo Realism is but the latest incarnation of American Scene painting, a latter day version of the Ashcan School..." writes Barbara Rose of 1970s art in her book *American Painting, the Twentieth Century* (Editions d'Art Albert Skira, Geneva, 1980). When by the end of the 1950s, Abstract Expressionism and other non-objective painting had exhausted its avantgarde identification, representational painting intended for the mass public, otherwise known as the common consumer, emerged through Pop Art of the 1960s and then during the 1970s with Photo Realism. Photo Realism, Hyper Realism, or Super Realism became very popular with the public. The glossy surfaces and cool imperson-

ality of the works of Charles Bell, Richard Estes (Cat. No. 81) and David Parrish (Cat. No. 123) were colourful and shining. Viewers were fascinated by the technical perfection, and delighted with an easy and straightforward visual message. Charles Bell was born in Tulsa, Oklahoma, in 1935. During the 1960s he lived and painted in California before settling in New York in 1967. His works were widely shown at exhibitions around the United States, Japan, New Zealand, and Canada during the heyday of Photo Realism. In 1977 alone, the year *Thunder Smash* was painted and first exhibited in New York, the artist had thirteen exhibitions, thus testifying to the wide popularity of Photo Realist paintings. In *Thunder Smash* reference is made to the popular pinball machines found in cafeterias, bars and gambling halls—a commonplace manufactured piece of mechanical toy for grown-ups. The icy perfection of

bright metallic colours and the reflective surfaces of plexiglass, chrome, plastic and glossy paint of this magnified machine delight and entertain. Bell began the series of "Pinball Machine" paintings, to which *Thunder Smash* belongs, in 1977.

Cat. No. **55**
Thomas Hart Benton (1889-1975)
The City (New York Scene), 1920
Oil on canvas, 85.5 × 65 cm
Signed with initials and dated
lower right:
".B.Th 20"
1975.22

Thomas Hart Benton was from rural western town of Neosho, Missouri. He studied painting in Paris from 1908 until settling in New York in 1912. He preferred an art of the people, for the people, based on American experiences. As such, Benton was a painter of the quintessential American scene. During the 1930s this tendency in art was called Regionalism. Benton came from a politically prominent family and communicating with the masses was considered important and natural to him. During the 1920s and 30s, Benton received many commissions for large murals. In his art, he voiced his ideas and visions with a strong focus on the agrarian and folkloric. After World War I, American artists struggled to cast off European influences, and to define a distinctly American Art. Just as the rural regions represented specific American cultural values and a refuge from the speed and intensity of the metropolis, the city was seen as a product of modern life, technology, energy and sophistication. These two ideas symbolised a unique, new American manifestation. *The City (New York Scene)*, with its stark contrasts, swirling curves and jagged skyline represents an image of a city complete with turmoil and energy. The painting represents Madison Square, located at the crossings of Broadway, Fifth Avenue, and Twenty-Fifth Street. The statue is of Governor William Seward by Randolph Rogers. Benton had planned to stay in New York until 1935 but, he began identifying himself more with rural America (see Cat. No. 56), and decided to move back permanently to his home state, settling in Kansas City.

Cat. No. 56
Thomas Hart Benton (1889-1975)
Pop and the Boys, 1963
Oil on canvas, 67.8 × 47.7
Signed and dated lower right:
"Benton 63"
1976.5

World War II changed both America and people's outlook. It was difficult for an artist of Thomas Hart Benton's very particular style—who persisted in promoting an optimistic view of America—to successfully propagate the same imagery within the new post-war reality. Public and critical taste turned dramatically from an interest in realistic works to a delight in abstract art. Benton despised abstract art. Although, he was pleased with the success of Jackson Pollock—one of his own pupils who had studied with him at the Art Students League from 1930 to 1933. Pollock's abstract drip paintings represented a strong reaction to Benton's teachings and initiated a new trend and fashion in American art (see Cat. Nos. 126-128). Benton, who was now regarded as old-fashioned, continued his work along the lines of the Regionalist movement established during the 1920s and 1930s. *Pop and the Boys* of 1963, is a variation on several compositions of the years 1928-32, depicting a group of farmers playing music outside a farmhouse.

Cat. No. **57**
Oscar Bluemner (1867-1938)
Red Towards Blue, 1933
Tempera on cardboard,
60 × 80 cm
Signed lower left:
"Blümnner" (all joined)
1973.54

German-born Oscar Bluemner was among the young artists who focused on the new issues in painting first introduced by the European Fauve, Cubist and Futurist artists that had been represented in the 1913 revolutionary New York Armory Show. In the Armory Show, Bluemner himself exhibited five paintings. His works hung in the American section which seemed very tame in comparison to that of the Europeans, where Marcel Duchamp's *Nude Descending a Staircase*, 1912, caused the greatest sensation. Bluemner's contribution to the advancement of modern art in America has never been fully appreciated. The training received as an architect before becoming a painter helped him formalise and structure pictorial representation in an increasingly reductive manner. This ability led him towards abstraction. His concern with colour theories, taken up during a European sojourn in 1912, intensified his preference for bright, simple, prismatic colours. Bluemner believed in the emotional and psychological significance of colours and explained that, to him, red represented the female, emotional and intuitive; and blue the male, intellectual forces of life. In the paintings executed right before his 1938 suicide, such as *Red Towards Blue*, and *Red and White*, 1934 (Cat. No. 57), Bluemner sets red up against blue in a highly abstract representation of a house and tree in a landscape. The barren tree against the house reflects the artist's loneliness and depression after his wife's death in 1926.

Cat. No. **58**
Oscar Bluemner (1867-1938)
Red and White, 1934
Tempera, 58.5 × 81.5 cm
Signed lower left:
"Blümner" (all joined)
1974.1

Oscar Bluemner, who stands out
as one of the pioneers of American Abstraction, moved to South
Braintree, Massachusetts, with
his two children after his wife's
death in 1926. The following decade was marked by financial strug-
gles and depression which eventually led to his suicide in 1938. Like
similar compositions of the time,
Red and White, 1934, depicts red
buildings, symbolizing perhaps
"home" as a female attribute, and a
cool blue church as a symbol of
man. The buildings are placed in a
white and blue snow-covered landscape with barren trees reaching
into the red sky. A sterile silence
pervades this cold and lonely place
reflecting Bluemner's sentiment.

Cat. No. **59**
Felix de Boeck (1898-?)
Abstract, 1921
Oil on masonite panel,
60 × 68 cm
Signed and dated upper right:
"Felix de Boeck 1921"
1978.82

Felix de Boeck was born in Dro-
genbos, Belgium, in 1898. He studied history of art at the University
of Brussels before becoming a
painter associated with Belgium's
young avant-garde movement.
During these years, 1916 to 1922,
de Boeck became friendly with
Fritz van den Berghe and Piet
Mondrian. He became influenced
by their ideas of a logical, geomet-
ric-abstract visual order in painting, exemplified in the works produced for the Dutch publication *De
Stijl*. De Boeck abandoned, around
1919, the Fauve technique in favour of Abstraction. In his first abstract compositions, the space between receding and intersecting
lines is coloured in subdued tonal
harmonies, which are very different from the bright primary colours of his De Stijl contemporaries. His works of the period can be
described as poetic abstractions
due to the effect of discrete balance
and harmony. *Abstract*, 1921, is a
composition from this initial phase
of the artist's experiments with
non-figurative painting. In this
work de Boeck stresses the diagonal lines and creates, at their in-
tersection in the central part of
the composition, a luminous focal
point which stands out as a vibrant
graphic symbol against the background of chromatically organised
earthen colours. De Boeck later
abandoned abstraction and returned to figurative painting of cityscapes, animals, and portraits.

Cat. No. 60
Charles Ephraim Burchfield
(1893-1967)
Haunted Evening, 19119
Watercolour on paper,
40.6 × 63.5 cm
Signed and dated lower right:
"C Burchfield 1919"
1978.20

In 1914, the young student of the
Cleveland School of Art, Charles
Ephraim Burchfield, noted in his
journals: "I hereby dedicate my
life and soul to the study and love
of nature with the purpose of
bringing it before the mass of unin-
terested public." The year after he
discarded academic practise and
proceeded to create astonishingly
expressive watercolours which
have always stood out as one of the
most isolated and original phenom-
ena in twentieth century American
painting. The works of 1915-21
combine powerful action and expressionism with draughtsmanship and decoration. What Burch-

field tries to express was moods,
emotions, and sensations derived
from intense observation of his
surroundings. When Burchfield
painted *Haunted Evening*, he was
going through a difficult two-year
period where a morbid feeling pervaded his views. He was drafted in
1918, and had spent six miserable
months at Camp Jackson, South
Carolina. Burchfield later said that
Haunted Evening was a reminis-
cence of his stay. "... A man coming home to his little cabin, carrying his sack of provender, fearful of
the eerie, haunted, woods that
stand behind his home, against a
lurid sunset sky." Another dismal
reference is made in his diary of
1919: "...a bent old man I saw drag-
ging a sack muttering and cackling
into a house that looked like a knot-
ted stump or the face of an owl."

Cat. No. **61**
Charles Ephraim Burchfield
(1893-1967)
Dream of a Storm at Dawn,
1963-66
Watercolour on paper,
76.2 × 102 cm
Signed with initials and dated
lower left: "CB (1963) 1966"
1981.26

Traditionally the work of Charles Ephraim Burchfield has been divided into three distinct phases: his early years (1915-21), when he painted romantic expressionist works such as *Haunted Evening*, 1919 (Cat. No. 60) at his home in Salem, Ohio; his middle years (1921-43), when he painted realistic visions of the American scene marked by a dreariness and solitude of small-town America; and his late years (1943-67), when he returned to fantasy and large expressionist landscape compositions using works from his youth for renewed creative inspiration.

The last five years of his life produced some of the most moving expressionist pictures, pervaded by a dream-like quality or actually based on dreams as in *Dream of a Storm at Dawn*. Burchfield believed that the subconscious surfaced in dreams to establish important harmony between mind, soul and nature. The mystic powers of the elemental forces of nature—of light and dark, of the sun, moon, the seasons of the year—reverberate forcefully in the universe of his last paintings. Burchfield alone carries through more than half of our century, the pantheist feeling of early nineteenth-century American landscape painting.

Cat. No. 62
Ilia Grigorievich Chashnik
(1902-1929)
Composition, c. 1924
Watercolour on paper, 14 × 10 cm
1976.18

A native of Liuzin (Lyucite), Lat-
via, Ilia Grigorievich Chashnik
joined the newly-founded Art
Practical Institute of Vitebsk, By-
elorussia after having studied a
few months at the Moscow Vkhutemas (Higher Art Technical Studios). This academy was first run
by Marc Chagall, and subsequently, in 1919, by Kazimir Malevich
(Cat. No. 103). In Vitebsk, the
young artist became one of the star
pupils and a close personal collab-
orator of Malevich, the founder
and leader of Suprematism. In the
years immediately before and after the Revolution of 1917, Suprematism became the primary
Avant-Garde style in Russia and
was totally associated with the
spirit of the Revolution in society

and the arts. Under the guidance
of Malevich, this movement grew
from being a spiritual, philosophi-
cal, artistic language into a univer-
sally adopted decorative style.
When Chashnik graduated from
the Vitebsk Institute in 1922, he
moved to Petrograd to work with
both Malevich and the celebrated
Lomonosov Porcelain factory.
Chashnik participated in the exhibitions organised by the 1920-22
Avant-Garde group Unovis (Affirmers of the New Art)—an association basically made up of Malevich's Vitebsk Art school students.
Chashnik became a member of the
Ginkhuk (State Institute of Artistic Culture) in 1923 and taught at
the State Institute of Art History
in Leningrad from 1926. He died of
appendicitis at the early age of
twenty-seven, leaving behind an
oeuvre of great importance in the
history of Russian Avant-Garde
and Abstract art. This small pencil
and watercolour composition from
around 1924 was probably among

the many designs for the decoration of porcelain which Chashnik
created for the Lomonosov Porcelain Factory in Petrograd. The
composition plays on two fan-like
movements; rectangular elements
emanate from the left as multico-
loured rays of different sizes flow
across the composition towards
the right. The porcelain designed
by Russian Avant-Garde artists
for the Lomonosov Porcelain Factory during the 1920s rank as the
most original experiments with domestic and industrial porcelain of
the twentieth century.

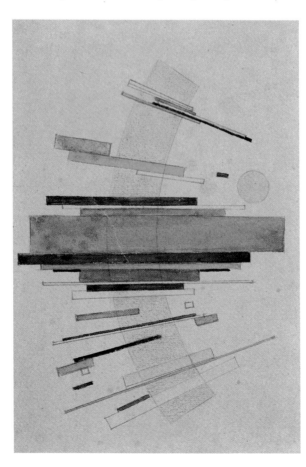

Cat. No. **63**
Ilia Grigorievich Chashnik
(1902-1929)
Suprematist Relief No. II, c. 1926
Oil paint on wood and glass,
82.8 × 62.3 cm
1976.13

The belief in progress, science, industry, and a new social system was the fundamental stimulus of Russian artistic creativity during the first three decades of this century. Artists saw themselves as powerful movers and shakers of a revived society. The sense of unlimited opportunities for re-shaping the environment according to new aesthetic yet functional ideals stimulated Russian Avant-Garde artists to experiment in all fields of artistic expression. In Russia, there was practically no tradition of sculpture. During the 1920s there grew, mainly out of Suprematism and Constructivism, a great many experiments with pictorial reliefs and spatial constructions;

incorporating such materials as wood, glass, cardboard, and metal. The reliefs translate the painted versions of rectangles, squares, lines, and circles of the Suprematist vocabulary—all in the reduced colour range originally invented by Malevich. These reliefs resemble architectural models for imaginary buildings and cities. To a great extent, Vladimir Tatlin's utopian architectural models designed for Monument to the III International (1919-20) initiated widespread experiments bordering between architecture and sculpture. *Suprematist Relief No. II* is one of a series of reliefs Ilia Grigorievich Chashnik began during the 1920s, first in Vitebsk and later in Petrograd. There are several versions and variants of *Suprematist Relief No. II*. This composition originally belonged to the family of the artist, whose son married the daughter of Nicolai Suetin, a fellow member of the Vitebsk Unovis group.

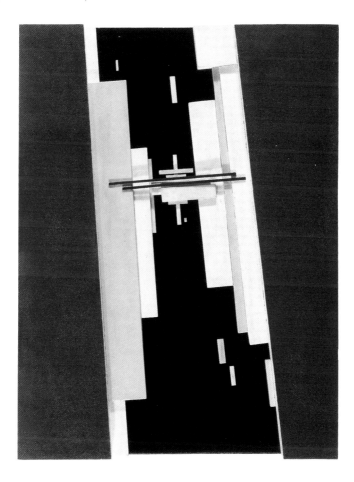

Cat. No. **64**
Giorgio de Chirico (1888-1978)
*Portrait of a Young Girl
with an Apple*, 1921
Oil on canvas, 41 × 30.5 cm
Signed and dated lower left:
"G. de Chirico 1921"
Inscribed lower right: "luglio 1940
- all'amico Rodolfo Siviero molto
cordialmente G. de Chirico"
1977.30

Giorgio de Chirico was born and
spent the greater part of his early
youth in Volos, Greece, where his
father, an Italian engineer, was
stationed. His earliest visual recollections were the sea, columns,
ruins, and sculptures of Greece.
When his father died in 1906, his
mother decided to send Giorgio
and his brother Andrea to study
painting and music in Munich.
During the two years he studied
there, de Chirico was particularly
influenced by the art of Arnold
Böcklin. From 1911-14 he lived in
Paris where he came in contact

with the circle of artists around the
poet Apollinaire. Since his childhood, de Chirico had suffered from
depression and melancholy. His
paintings were imbued with a very
particular and paralleled atmosphere of loneliness and alienation.
For most of his long, artistic career, the recurrent elements of his
imagery were statues, arcades, fa-
cades, the sea, the dressmaker's
mannequin, and an absurd won-
derland perspective. During the
period from 1919 to 1922 when he
lived and worked in Ferrara, Italy,
de Chirico started referring to his
works as metaphysical paintings.
This term which was to suggest
the kind of universal symbolic val-
ue of the motifs he employed a decade before Surrealism took up the
same ideas. From 1919 to 1922 de
Chirico was very involved with the
publication of the art monthly *Valori Plastici*, and began an intense
study of the great Renaissance
masters—the main inspiration for
a series of portraits executed dur-

ing those years. *Young Girl with
an Apple*, 1921, belongs to this
phase of de Chirico's work. The
painting at one time belonged to
the journalist, maecenas, and publisher of *Valori Plastici*, Mario
Broglio, who is known to have
strongly supported avant-garde
art.

Cat. No. **65**
Giorgio de Chirico (1888-1978)
*The Solitary Archaeologist
(L'Archeologo Solitario)*, 1966
Oil on canvas, 50 × 40 cm
Signed lower right:
"G. de Chirico"
1974.11

When Giorgio de Chirico returned to Paris in 1924, he was celebrated as the grand precursor of the Surrealist movement. The haunted, dream-like compositions of de Chirico's work of the previous decade were an important source of inspiration in the development of Surrealism during the 1920s. His own works of the 1920s, however, differed markedly both stylistically and iconographically from that of the Surrealist painters. By 1926, he broke with the group. De Chirico's greatest contribution to art of this century lies in his production up until this moment; although he continued to work steadily over the next four decades in Rome on murals, theatre designs, and paintings, the impact of his art tapered off. The mannequin or robot-like figure in *The Solitary Archaeologist*, first appeared in de Chirico's work in 1916, and was used throughout his career. The empty face of the figure imparts no expression, and the viewer focuses instead on the architectural fragments from classical antiquity piled in the archaeologist's torso.

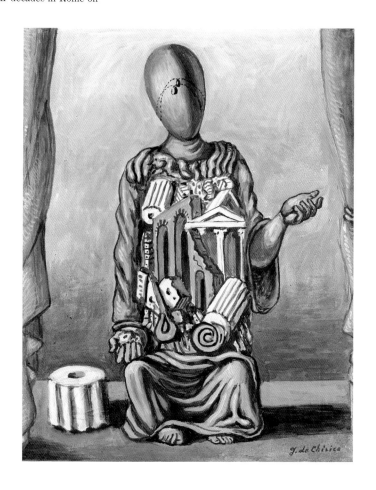

Cat. No. **66**
Robert Courtright (1926-)
Untitled, 1977
Collage of brown papers
with letters, 79 × 81 cm
Signed and dated
lower left:
"Courtright '77"
1977.92

Robert Courtright, originally from
Sumter, South Carolina made
Opio, France his home and chose to
live there for the reason that he
loved the Mediterranean Romanesque architecture of the south-
ern area. His early works, after
taking classes at the Art Students
League in New York, were collages of Romanesque towers and
churches from Rome and Rapallo,
Italy (1950s). During the next decade, Courtright's collages—the
technique used exclusively by the
artist—became increasingly abstract, taking on the austere aspect of walls of ancient stones and
bricks. Courtright found, as he
said, "an affinity between the ver-
tical-horizontal necessity of buildings and the cut rectangular shape
in which paper usually presents itself." Courtright assembled his
collages of the 1970s and early
80s—of which *Untitled* and *Navy
Blue Tread* are typical examples—
from rectangles or squares of paper, like bricks in a wall. The artist
has said of his methods: "Collage is
frequently composed of paper or
other material with different histo-
ries, other reasons for existing,
which has little to do with their
present function. Obviously little
in a work of art is completely new:
most has been passed on, handed
down, refound, rescued, and very
often, and this is particularly true
in my work, the materials retain
something of their earlier existence which, though submerged, ultimately contribute to the effect of
the whole." ("Twelve American
Masters of Collage," Andrew Cris-
po Gallery, New York, November
17-December 30, 1977).

Cat. No. **67**
Robert Courtright (1926-)
Navy Blue Tread, 1983
Collage, acrylic and paper
mounted on board,
172.5 × 179.1 cm
Signed and dated lower right:
"Courtright '83"
Signed and dated on verso
top right: "Courtright '83"
1983.24

Cat. No. 68
Stuart Davis (1894-1964)
Tao Tea Balls and Teapot, 1924
Oil on canvas, 46 × 61 cm
Signed and dated lower right:
"Stuart Davis '24"
1983.3

The career of Stuart Davis engaged every major development in American twentieth-century painting from Ashcan School Realism to Pop Art. Davis, who studied in New York with Robert Henri (Cat. No. 88) from 1910, considered the Armory Show of 1913 the most important event in his formative years; it started him working on Cubist compositions. During the 1920s Davis emerged as one of the most important of the younger generation artists. 1922 was the year he truly assimilated Cubism and, by 1924, he had developed the planar, angular flattened picture space with a strong emphasis on line, which was to characterise his art henceforth. First came a series of Picasso-inspired collages which allowed him to simplify and forms into flat, cut out shapes. The Cubist still-lifes that followed in 1922-24 are among the most original works in American Cubism—some of them embracing total abstraction. Within his astonishing production of these years *Tao Tea Balls and Teapot*, is a conventional still-life with Cubist elements, and less provocatively experimental as some of the other compositions. The division of the surface into three rectangular planes with their individual "wall paper" patterns occurs also in *Edison Mazda* of 1924 (The Metropolitan Museum of Art, New York). The objects are clearly lined up on the table, each on a planar field of shadow; glass and lemon—archetypical Cubist still-life elements are firm, prominent and naturalistic. Great prominence is placed on the letters of the label on the tea canister. This work points in the direction of the Pop Art of Roy Lichtenstein.

Cat. No. **69**
Charles Demuth (1883-1935)
Church in Provincetown, No. 2,
1919
Watercolour on paper,
44.5 × 34.5 cm
Signed and dated lower left:
"C. Demuth-1919-"
1973.62

Charles Demuth is a central figure
in the group of avant-garde artists
who pioneered Modernism in
America during the first highly innovative decades of the twentieth
century. He was born and died
in his Lancaster, Pennsylvania
home. Demuth spent important
years of his training as an artist in
Paris, first in 1904, then for a year
in 1907, and again in 1912 until 1914.
During his visits to Paris, he made
lasting friendships with the collec-
tors Gertrude and Leo Stein and
Marsden Hartley, and met John
Marin (Cat. Nos. 108, 109), whom
he greatly admired. It was back in
New York in 1915-16 where he

came in contact with the French
artists Marcel Duchamp, Albert
Gleizes, Francis Picabia (Cat. no.
125), and the American artist,
Georgia O'Keeffe. Each of the
aforementioned artists exercised
tremendous influence on his work.
By this time, Demuth had already
presented several one man shows
at the Charles Daniel Gallery,
New York. He was known for the
sheer brilliance of his command of
the watercolour technique. The
summer of 1916, which Demuth
spent in Provincetown in the company of his artist friend Marsden
Hartley, is when Demuth explored
a Cubist derived compositional device, later called Precisionism — or
Cubist-Realism. This device grew
out of the moderately fragmented
Cubist landscapes by Gleizes, and
took elements from Italian Futurism and Russian Avant-Garde
painting. In *Church in Provincetown, No. 2* of 1919, Demuth experimented with predominantly recti-
linear forms, painted in clear un-

mixed colour pools. The result is a
personal interpretation of Cubism
where the artist couples a stylized
geometry with a soft, diffused ra-
diance. This technique was particularly suited during that time for
architectural scenes, and depictions of factories and industrial
buildings, all which came to represent the age of the machine, progress and prosperity. The years
1916-22, when Demuth painted
these Cubist styled landscapes are
considered highly important to his
artistic development.

Cat. No. **70**
Charles Demuth (1883-1935)
Red and Yellow Tulips, 1933
Watercolour on paper,
24.7 × 35 cm
Signed and dated lower right:
"C Demuth 33"
1979.33

Charles Demuth experimented
with various types of floral watercolour compositions during the
1910s: soaking the paper with melting, burning colour zones or adopt-
ing a delicate oriental compositional harmony. In 1922-23, shortly after his fourth and final trip to Europe, flowers and still-lifes became
his major motif. It is within this
genre that Demuth was to receive
his first awards in 1926 and 1927.
Red and Yellow Tulips, and *Zinnias* are two late flower compositions executed just two years before Demuth's death. Leaving
much of the white paper bare, Demuth works with intense colours
within delicate pencil outlines.

Cat. No. **71**
Charles Demuth (1883-1935)
Zinnias, 1933
Watercolour on paper,
33 × 25.5 cm
Signed and dated
left lower centre:
"C Demuth '33"
1979.21

Cat. No. **72**
Walter Dexel (1890-1973)
Skyscraper (Hochhaus), 1923
Oil on canvas, 65 × 46 cm
Signed and dated lower right:
"WDexel23"
1978.76

Walter Dexel was born in 1890 in Munich, Germany. He studied art history at the Universities of Munich, and Jena. From 1916 to 1928 he directed the exhibition activities of the Kunstverein Jena, and during these years had the opportunity to focus on high caliber German avant-garde artists. Among the many exhibitions he organised were shows of the groups Die Brücke, Blaue Reiter, Dada (1922), the German Constructivists (1923) and the famous Bauhaus School. Members of this local school included Johannes Itten (Cat. No. 93), Wassily Kandinsky, Oskar Schlemmer, and Paul Klee. Their works and that of their students were represented in Dexel shows such as "New German Architecture" (1924) and "New Advertisement" (1927). As a painter he joined the Constructivists, exhibiting at der Sturm Gallery in Berlin in 1918, 1920 and again in 1925. During the 1920s he also participated in exhibitions in Paris and Moscow. Around 1920 his paintings became increasingly geometric. By 1922, they were totally non-objective. For a period Dexel associated himself with the De Stijl group which Bauhaus member Theo van Doesburg was heading during the years 1921-23. Some other artists belonging to this group were Karl Peter Röhl (Cat. No. 133), the Dutch artist Cesar Domela (Cat. No. 73), Kurt Schwitters, and Lajos Kassák (Cat. No. 95). All, like Dexel, also joined the "Neue Werbegestalter" group of commercial artists. Dexel was very interested in typography, commercial art, visual communication and graphics. He taught at the Magdeburg Applied Arts and Handicrafts School from 1928. In 1933 Dexel stopped painting altogether, and only resumed doing so in 1961, almost thirty years later. Labelled a degenerate artist by the Nazis, he was expelled from his post in Magdeburg in 1935, and forbidden to teach in 1942. When he took up painting again in 1961, Dexel still adhered to the constructivist principles characterising his works of the 1920s.

In 1969 several group shows on the theme of national Constructivists started taking place in Germany. Dexel was rediscovered and hailed as one of the only three true German Constructivists, the others being Willi Baumeister and Carl Buchheister. Works by Dexel are in museums all over Germany but represented in few foreign museums apart from the Metropolitan Museum in New York, and the Thyssen-Bornemisza Collection. The painting *Skyscraper* belongs to Dexel's development of street scenes and architectural city views. It is governed by a calculated organisation of geometric forms which parallels architectural thinking. What distinguishes Dexel from other Constructivists is the suggestive effect of his colours: modulated surfaces and a variation of hues balanced in aesthetic harmony. Dexel published several books on Handicrafts: *Unknown Handicrafts*, and *German Handicrafts*, *Household Utensils of*

Central Europe. From 1942 until his death in 1973 Dexel lived and worked in Werbegestalter, Brunswick, establishing the Formsammlung der Stadt Braunschweig (1942-55). *Skyscraper*, painted in 1923, was first exhibited in 1974 in the first retrospective exhibition of the artist's work at Kestner Gesellschaft, in Hannover, the year after his death.

Cat. No. 73
Cesar Domela (1900-1992)
Composition No. 5 M,
Lozange 1926
Oil on canvas, 60 × 60 cm
Signed and dated on verso:
C. Domela. Paris 1926"
1979.83

The striking similarity of *Composition No. 5 M, Lozange* with works by Piet Mondrian immediately place the Dutch-born artist Cesar Domela with the De Stijl group named after the art magazine founded by Theo van Doesburg in 1917. Mondrian's theories of Neo-Plasticism or New Forming, dominated the painting, architecture and design of De Stijl artists. Domela had met Mondrian and Theo van Doesburg in Paris in 1924 and joined De Stijl, to which also Karl Peter Röhl (Cat. No. 133) belonged—two years before *Composition No. 5 M, Lozange*. Typically, these abstract geometrical paintings contain a grid of

straight, black lines dividing the surface of a square white canvas into rectangles and squares of different sizes—some of which are coloured in unmodulated primary colours of blue, red or yellow. Domela turned the canvas of *Composition No. 5 M, Lozange* on a corner to form a lozange—a feature also used by Mondrian. Domela, who was self-taught, spent the years from 1919 to 1923 in Ascona, Switzerland, where Arthur Segal had lived. When Domela went to Berlin in 1923, he was introduced to Segal through a mutual painter friend from Ascona. Segal received him very kindly, and offered him to come to his school to paint anytime he wanted, Domela would not have to follow the classes and pay for the tuition. In an interesting interview given by Domela on the occasion of the great Segal retrospective exhibition in Cologne in 1987, Domela described his Berlin years and the great difference between his paintings and

those of his mentor. This difference is obvious when comparing this work by Domela with Segal's composition *Bridge*, 1921 (Cat. No. 138). Domela's first abstract compositions date from 1923, and were exhibited in Berlin with the Novemberguppe and the Abstrakten Hannover group. At the same time he joined, with Walter Dexel (Cat. No. 72) and Lajos Kassák (Cat. No. 95), the Neue Werbegestalter group of commercial graphic artists. By the time Domela settled in Paris in 1933, he had turned to compositions of swirling lines and circular shapes, often used in assemblages and collages. In Paris he joined Abstraction-Creation and started, with Hans Arp and Sophie Tauber, the publication *Plastique*. During the 1950s he received several official commissions for large murals in his home country. In 1987 a retrospective exhibition of his works toured Paris, Grenoble and Amsterdam.

Cat. No. 74
Guy Pène du Bois (1884-1958)
Le Viol, c. 1927
Oil on canvas, 101.5 × 76.5 cm
Signed lower left:
"Guy Pène du Bois"
1979.85

Guy Pène du Bois was a student of
Robert Henri (Cat. No. 88) at the
New York School of Art where he
had been studying since 1899. The
teaching of Henri marked a shift
into Realism and focused on re-
porting the reality of daily life.
Henri and some of his students, including Guy Pène du Bois, broke
with the traditional exhibition or-
ganisations governed by the National Academy in 1908. Henri
organised his own exhibition with
an independent group called The
Eight including, among others,
Ernest Lawson (Cat. No. 33) and
Edward Hooper (Cat. Nos. 90-92).
The "Exhibition of Paintings and
Drawings by Contemporary Artists" took place on Forty-Second
Street in New York, with The
Eight. Most of these artists had
backgrounds or part-time jobs in
newspaper and magazine illustration. The objective of this employment was to tell or illustrate sto-
ries. After a stay in Paris, du Bois
worked from 1906 for the *New
York American*, and the *New York
Tribune*, first as a reporter and later as an art critic. He did all this
while establishing himself as a
painter. Du Bois lived with his
family in France from 1924-30. *Le
Viol*, with its French title meaning
rape or violation, was probably
painted during this period. Whether or not an actual event inspired
this nocturnal scene is not known.
The woman is, however, clearly
being dragged off in a rough manner to the seedy hotel, indicated by
the sign rooms in the background.

Cat. No. **75**
Guy Pène du Bois (1884-1958)
42nd Street, 1945
Oil on canvas, 81.5 × 66 cm
Signed lower right:
"Guy Pène du Bois"
1981.29

Guy Pène du Bois taught at various institutions from 1920 through
the 1930s. During the 1940s, he received numerous awards his health
started deteriorating influencing
not only his production, but also
his outlook on life. His works were
not selling well anymore, times
and styles were changing with
World War II, and the Realism of
du Bois was becoming old-fashioned as Abstraction made a
breakthrough. In *42nd Street*, du
Bois observes the world in busy
mid-town Manhattan. He concen-
trates on the women who are fash-
ionably dressed. Du Bois' women
have the impersonal expression
and shape of long-legged, tight-
waisted wax models.

Cat. No. 76
(Kseniia) Xenia Vladimirovna Ender (1895-1955)
Composition, 1918
Oil on cardboard, 48.5 × 61.5 cm
1980.19

Xenia Vladimirovna Ender studied from 1917 to 1922 at the Petrograd Free Art Studios in the department of Spatial Realism under the direction of Mikhail Matiushin. Matiushin was an accomplished painter, musician, publisher, teacher, and friend of Malevich (Cat. No. 103), who at the time was a dominant figure in the circles where Ender received her artistic formation. Malevich and Matiushin were both intensively engaged in theoretical analysis of modern painting. In fact, Mutiushin had published the famous Malevich essay *From Cubism and Futurism to Suprematism*, which accompanied the 1915 "Last Futurist Exhibition 0.10" of St. Petersburg. Matiushin's non-objective form of painting was, however, rooted in the observation of nature and attempted what he called a "widening of vision." Matiushin named his theory "Zorved" (literally See-Know). Ender was influenced by the ideas of Matiushin, and dedicated herself from 1923-26 to assisting him in development of the Zorved theories in the department of Organic Culture at Ginkhuk in Petrograd/Leningrad. She continued to be very close to Matiushin until he died in 1934. Ender was active as an artist for just a little over ten years. Serious illness, however, forced her to stop painting altogether. During the years when she was most productive she participated in the "Exhibition of Paintings by Petrograd Artists of All Directions" (1923), and in the 14th Venice Biennale (1924). *Composition* dates from the beginning of her student years when she was immersed in abstract compositions in which she explored the energies of colour, and the nature of cosmic forces. *Composition* appears as a cosmic distribution of molecular matter of different weights, volumes, and speeds, as indicated by colour and size and, thus, organised by centrifugal force. The compositional technique can be likened to Futurist compositions of Giacomo Balla and Umberto Boccioni.

Cat. No. 77
(Kseniia) Xenia Vladimirovna
Ender (1895-1955)
Untitled, 1918
Oil on cardboard, 42.7 × 62 cm
1978.77

Untitled is another example of Xenia Vladimirovna Ender's experiments with non-objective form as a
young student at the Petrograd
Free Art Studios.
Painted in 1918 like *Composition*,
the present work explores the visual language of Malevich's (Cat.
No. 103) Suprematist compositions
with bold, planar geometric shapes
floating in a spatial void.

Cat. No. 78
Max Ernst (1891-1976)
The Sea (La Mer), 1924
Oil on canvas, 46.5 × 38.1 cm
Signed lower left: "max ernst"
Titled lower right: "la mer"
1976.6

German born Max Ernst was one of the most influential artists in Europe between World War I and World War II. He was a founding member of the 1919 Cologne Dada movement, and participated in the creation of Parisian Surrealism in 1924. The artist was gifted with a vivid imagination. The range of styles and techniques Ernst explored in the course of his long, active career was extraordinary. From 1911 to the outbreak of the war, when he served in the German army, Ernst was in touch with August Macke (Cat. No. 102) and the painters of the groups Das Junge Rheinland and Blaue Reiter. When he started painting again after the war in 1919, Giorgio de

Chirico's "metaphysical" compositions — which had been reproduced in periodicals such as the Italian monthly *Valori Plastici* — had a significant impact on him. Ernst absorbed Dada ideas of shock and negation and proceeded as a Surrealist to explore dreams and other manifestations of the unconscious. He found artistic expression in the collages he began in 1919. From 1922, Ernst lived in Paris and was actively involved with the Surrealist group through their first exhibition in 1925. Other artists included in the show were de Chirico (Cat. Nos. 64, 65), André Masson (Cat. No. 112), Man Ray (Cat. No. 106), and Joan Miró. Ernst's art continued to retain, however, an intellectual affinity with the Dada spirit of puzzling visual constellations and juxtapositions. In the composition *The Sea*, the straight line of the horizon sharply divides sea and sky into two sections. The focus of the composition is the star which has plunged into the black

depths of the sea and, from there, it beams and vibrates. The straight lines dividing sea from sky, and the different blues of the layers of the atmosphere above sea-level are contrasted with the shimmering concentric circles of light emanated by the soft glowing star. The circular shape, the disc, the wheel, or the sun occurs frequently in Ernst's compositions from the beginning of the 1920s onward.

Cat. No. **79**
Max Ernst (1891-1976)
*Loplop Presents the Beautiful
Season (Loplop Présente la Belle
Saison),* c. 1930
Oil on canvas, 38 × 46 cm
Signed lower right: "max ernst"
1977.107

Recalling his childhood, Max
Ernst mentioned that his dear
friend the parrot Hornebom died
the same night in 1906 when his little sister Loni was born. Somehow
this coincidence fostered in him a
lasting, irrational sensation that
the spirit of the bird had taken
home in a human being. From then
on, he used birds as the symbol of
man. Between 1930 and 1933,
Ernst produced a large series
(about seventy pieces) of collages
and oil paintings—each revolving
around the mythical bird Loplop.
This bird became a metaphor of the
painter himself, or possibly his al-
ter ego. The majority of the compositions are titled "Loplop pre-

sents...," and show either a bird or
a stylized version of a bird holding
a framed image. That is, the compositions provide a picture within a
picture. The bird which is quite
prominent in the earliest of the
compositions is reduced, by the
last of the works, to the most mini-
malist of signs; almost an abstract
hieroglyph. In *Loplop Presents the
Beautiful Season,* the white bird
presents a painting of a partially
disintegrated horse or mastodon.
The skeleton-like horse of the present composition also appears in
the collage *The Great Mastodon,*
or *Loplop Presents Paul Eluard,*
of 1932, in which Ernst has incorporated a nineteenth century engraving of the skeleton with the
caption *The Great Mastdon.*

Cat. No. 80
Max Ernst (1891-1976)
The Red Sun, 1957
Oil on canvas, 31 × 41.4 cm
Signed lower right: "max ernst"
1971.5

When World War II began in 1939, Max Ernst, German by birth, was interned in France as an enemy alien. He managed to escape to the United States in 1941 and lived there until 1953. A number of other Dada and Surrealist artists, including André Breton, André Masson (Cat. No. 112), Man Ray (Cat. No. 106), and Marcel Duchamp spent the war years in exile in New York. Here they were gathered in what finally became the new centre of Surrealist activity. Ernst missed the café-life and atmosphere of Paris. He wrote that it was hard being an expatriate painter because "there were artists in New York, but no art." Ernst had by 1925 invented the method of rubbing or "frottage"—exploiting

the motifs that would surface by chance when rubbing planks of wood, leaves, sackcloth, etc. This method, which paralleled Masson's use of automatic writing, would subsequently develop in the 1940s into various techniques of blotting, staining, and smearing called "Decalcomania," and another new technical process called "Oscillation." In Oscillation a tin can of paint with a hole in its base is swung rhythmically from a string over a canvas laid on the floor. This formula, first used by Ernst in 1942, preceded the drip paintings of Jackson Pollock (Cat. Nos. 126-128). It is known that both Robert Motherwell and Pollock had seen and had been intrigued by these types of painting. Ernst moved to a ranch in Arizona in 1946 and stayed there until his 1953 return to France. In 1954, Ernst was awarded the Grand Prix for Painting at the Venice Biennale. His fellow Surrealists Joan Miró and Hans Arp won the other prizes. He

was ultimately excluded by Breton from the rather old Surrealist group, and spent his last years in France involved in experiments. Sculpture played great importance in his work, and the titles of his paintings like *The Red Sun* show that his imagination was still essentially Surrealist. *The Red Sun* of 1957 is related to a series of landscapes begun in 1952—while Ernst was still living in Arizona—where the sun is setting or rising over the horizon.

Cat. No. 81
Richard Estes (1936-)
Hotel Lucerne, 1976
Oil on canvas, 122.3 × 153 cm
Signed as a blue sign
at right of pub sign:
"RICHARD ESTES"
1982.14

While the 1960s in America produced a cacophony of post-abstractionist styles, of which Pop Art was the most popular, Richard Estes shared little with the prevailing trends except that he used everyday imagery like the Pop artists. After moving to New York from Chicago in 1959, Estes worked for about ten years as a graphic artist to make a living. When Richard Estes talks about his working methods he says that in 1965 he was just walking around the city photographing things and people, using these photos to create high-information representation of New York urban scenes. On this basis, his art has been called

Realism or Super Realism, Photo Realism or Contemporary Realism, but is more accurately his personal reflection on the reality of life in the generic city of our century. Estes acknowledges to follow the tradition of Thomas Eakins and Edward Hopper (Cat. Nos. 90-92). Fascinated with the interplay of reality and reflection, Estes paints the architecture, storefronts, street furniture, and signage of New York, dominated by the high clear New York sky. *Hotel Lucerne* which depicts Manhattan's Amsterdam Avenue and West Seventy-Ninth Street, where the Hotel Lucerne occupies the corner above the now discontinued Hardware Housewares store, was first exhibited at the Sidney Janis Gallery in 1976 under the title *Phone Phone*. This original title relates more accurately to the painting, and refers to the duplication of various pictorial features within the composition. Not only are twin phone booths prominently dis-

played right in the center of the composition, but a number of other pictorial details such as the firebox and the group of a yellow estate car, a black and a white car, and buildings along the east side of West End Avenue are seen twice because of the artist's clever handling of window reflection. It is unusual for Richard Estes, one of the most outstanding Photo Realists of the 1970s and 80s, to incorporate figures in his street scenes, such as the two persons crossing Amsterdam Avenue. In fact, the yellow taxicab driving-down West Seventy-Ninth Street has but a phantom driver at the wheel. Although most of the brownstone buildings along Amsterdam Avenue have since been demolished and replaced by skyscrapers with the ongoing metamorphosis of the New York skyline, the wealth and variety of street signage is so indigenous to the atmosphere of New York City that it will be familiar to anyone who has ever been there.

Cat. No. **82**
Alexandra Alexandrovna Exter
(1882-1949)
Two Women in a Garden, 1927
Oil on canvas, 85 × 70 cm
Signed lower right: "A Exter."
1976.78

Alexandra Alexandrovna Exter is one of the female artists who made a considerable impact on Russian Avant-Garde art during the 1910s and 1920s. Once she graduated from the Kiev Art Institute in 1907, Exter began taking several trips to Western Europe where she came into contact with Pablo Picasso, Georges Braque and the Italian Futurists. Exter became an important transmitter of the latest trends and happenings in Paris for her country. Until she moved to St. Petersburg in 1912, she exhibited in various Kiev, Moscow and St. Petersburg Avant-Garde exhibitions. During the years 1914-21 she continued experimenting with Cubism, Futur-

ism and the abstraction of Suprematism and Constructivism. Exter participated in the Avant-Garde exhibitions "Tramway V," "Shop" (1915-16) and the famous main Constructivist exhibition "5 × 5 = 25" of 1921. She also had the opportunity to work with Alexander Tairov on the costumes and sets for several performances of the Chamber Theatre Moscow (1915-23). During the early years of the twentieth century, Russian intellectuals gave more respect to the conventionality of theatre and many Avant-Garde artists worked at different stages of their careers for theatre and film. Exter's involvement with theatre costume and stage sets continued even after she emigrated to Paris in 1924. Both her costume designs and Cubist/Dadaist/Constructivist marionettes which she executed for a film by Peter Gad in Paris in 1926 represent a great contribution to scenic art. In these puppets, Exter reveals a gift for sculptural inven-

tion. The artist set up her own art school in 1918 (Odessa/Kiev) where she introduced highly original teaching methods. In Paris where she lived until the end of her life she continued to teach at Léger's "Académie d'Art Contemporain" (1925-30). Exter had her first one-woman exhibition in 1927 at the gallery "Der Sturm" in Berlin, the year *Two Women in a Garden* was painted. In Moscow, Exter was called the "Russian Léger," but much of her work represents a synthesis of Cubist, Futurist and Suprematist-Constructivist elements. The curved shading or the modulation of surface with which Léger gives volume to body also defines the contours of Exter's red and blue women in this composition. Exter uses more lively and saturated colours than the somber, muted, tonal ones dominating Constructivist works. During the 1930s and 40s, Exter resolved to work primarily on book illustrations and other various commercial projects.

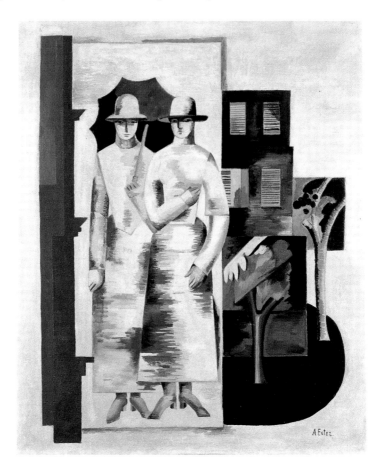

Cat. No. 83
Lucian Freud (1922-)
Still Life (Quinces), 1981-82
Oil on canvas, 16.5 × 22 cm
1984.22

Lucian Freud—grandson of Sigmund Freud—is one of the greatest living Realist painters. He was born in Berlin but the family moved to London in 1933 when Hitler became Chancellor and anti-semitism was escalating. Freud's juvenile works of the mid-1940s reveal some relationship to the Surrealism of Giorgio de Chirico (Cat. No. 64, 65) and Joan Miró, although the artist later said that "the rigidity of Surrealism, its rigid dogma of irrationality, seemed unduly limiting." In Freud's oeuvre, the portraits and nudes are so striking and so dominant that they appear to define his entire output. Freud, however, has always drawn and painted still-lifes of flowers and plants but is also known to depict animals and

fruits. Though few in comparison to Freud's figures, his still-life compositions add an enriching dimension to his portraits and nudes. The surfaces of Freud's still-life objects are painted like the flesh of his nudes: soft and sensual. The still lifes are small in dimension and observed at close range like this still life of quinces, painted in 1981-82. Freud delights in the physical quality of paint, material, flesh, and the bulging roundness of shapes. His quinces look enticingly fresh and juicy. *Still Life (Quinces)* is a fine example of a classical still-life painting.

Cat. No. 84
Lucian Freud (1922-)
Portrait of Baron H. H. Thyssen-Bornemisza (Man in a Chair),
1983-85
Oil on canvas, 120 × 100 cm
1985.19

"In 'normal' portraiture, a tacit agreement between painter and subject allows the sitter to mask himself and project this mask—of success, of dignity, of beauty, of role, upon the world. But here the face with its lowered eyes and eyelids is caught in a moment between reflection and self-projection. It is as naked as a hand." This analysis by Robert Hughes in his introduction to the catalogue of the large Lucian Freud exhibition which was shown in four countries in 1987-89, poignantly describes the *Portrait of Baron H. H. Thyssen-Bornemisza (Man in a Chair)*, which is one of two portraits commissioned by Baron Thyssen-Bornemisza from Lucian Freud, and

executed during the years 1981-85. In 1952 Freud created the outstanding portrait of painter friend Francis Bacon (Tate Gallery, London), followed by a series of portraits over the next three decades which can be considered masterpieces in the history of portraiture. Almost all of Freud's paintings are portraits, even the monumental nudes of the 1960's, 70s and 80s, he often calls "naked portraits." Freud's nudes do not adhere to conventional idealised vision of flawless youth and beauty; they are human, and strangely enough make the viewer uncomfortable.

Cat. No. **85**
Domenico Gnoli (1933-1970)
The Temple (Il Tempio), 1960
Oil on canvas, 99 × 79 cm
Signed and dated lower right:
"D. Gnoli 60"
1979.58

In a 1964 conversation with the collector Claude Spaak in Rome—a few years before the artist's premature death Domenico Gnoli explained his orientation in art: "My first sympathies were with the group of Metaphysical painters Carrà, Morandi: I presented, interpreted and stylized an object... Then came Pop Art where the object—vulgarised—was deprived of magic. I chose another road. Today I am interested in the object: the tablecloth, the dress, a piece of furniture, but I no longer deform it. On the contrary, I isolate it with extreme precision..." In another interview in New York in 1968, Gnoli said: "...I am metaphysical in the sense that I work towards a style of painting which is not eloquent, which is immobile and atmospheric, which is fed on static situations..." Gnoli, who moved repeatedly throughout his short life, spent the years 1957-62 in New York, where he became a friend of, among others, Ben Shahn (Cat. No. 141), and Saül Steinberg (Cat. No. 144). At the young age of thirty he was already established as one of the world's finest illustrators, and had worked for *Fortune*, *Holiday*, *Life*, *Show*, *Glamour*, *Sports Illustrated* and *Horizon*. Gnoli's focus on the object as subject matter led to comparison with American Pop Art of the 1960s, but his pictorial representation lay in the realm of Magic Realism. From around 1952, deserted piazzas and monumental antique buildings appeared in Gnoli's work, characterized by the same "absence of presence" of people as the great metaphysical compositions of Giorgio de Chirico earlier in the century. *The Temple*, painted in 1960, during the same year, and in the same style of *The Red Colosseum* (Collection of Mr. and Mrs. Robert Melville, London) belongs to this series. In both paintings, the Classical monuments fill the composition with a solidity and sculptural density.

Cat. No. 86
James Havard (1937-)
Sacred Circle, 1977
Acrylic, charcoal, and airbrush on
canvas, 153 × 167.5 cm
Titled upper center:
"Sacred"
Titled upper right:
"Sacred Circle"
Signed and dated lower right:
"Havard 77"
1977.95

James Havard was born in Galveston, Texas, in 1937. His training as an artist was at the Atelier Chapman Kelly, Dallas, Texas, from 1960. It was there that he had his first one-man exhibition in 1963. He enrolled at the Pennsylvania Academy of Fine Arts, Philadelphia, in 1965 and was awarded the "First Purchase Prize" of the "Drawing Society Traveling National Exhibition," Philadelphia Museum in that same year. Several exhibitions followed during the mid- and late-1960s, but it was from 1970 onward that Havard exhibited at a growing number of museums all over the United States. He was first represented abroad in 1974 at the Basel International Art Fair in Switzerland, and subsequently, in 1975 at Nordjyllands Kunstmuseum in Aalborg, Denmark. Apart from these rare appearances in an international context, Havard is exclusively associated with the American contemporary art scene. Together with a small group of artists, Havard belongs stylistically to the Abstract Illusionism movement, a colourful variant of Abstract Expressionism and Photo Realism of the 1970s and 80s. Abstract Illusionism implies trompe-l'oeil effects with non-figurative painterly elements. The purpose of trompe-l'oeil painting is traditionally to deceive the eye into perceiving a flat, two-dimensional surface as a space with objects: to fool the viewer that a depicted space and object is "real," to tempt the viewer to touch the painting to see if it is "real." As a movement, Abstract Illusionism is little known outside the United States and is limited to the 1970s and early 80s. *Sacred Circle* creates a puzzling but extremely convincing illusion that certain compositional elements, mainly shapes that seem to have been squeezed out of the paint tube directly onto the canvas, seem to float across an ambiguous space, casting shadows on the lower levels of the picture surface. An example is the "sacred" circle in yellow located in the upper part of the painting. Shading, shadows, overlapping forms, and curved canvas edges all work together in creating an illusion of space and a suggestion that this space extends past the surface towards the viewer. Likewise, an iridescent light created by working with airbrush, emanates through paint layers, as if the painting was lit from a source inside the composition.

Cat. No. 87
Al Held (1928-)
Solar Wind VI, 1974
Acrylic on canvas, 183 × 152.5 cm
1977.96

When Al Held saw the drip paintings of Jackson Pollock (Cat. Nos. 126-128) in New York in 1949, where he was studying at the Art Students League, he was initially impressed by the vitality of Action Painting. He was, however, also among the first American artists to react against the unstructured look and ambiguous space of Action Painting later in the 1950s. Held turned to orderly, discrete, legible shapes painted with tight, meticulous brushstrokes. In the 1960s and 70s—during the years when he was Professor of Painting at Yale University (1962-80)—his work assumed monumental proportions and his forms became increasingly bold and dramatic. Held used computer generated images to suggest apparently infinite vis-tas, complex foreshortening and scale changes all of which produce an eerie sensation of unnatural three-dimensionality, sometimes referred to as Abstract Illusionism. For twelve years, during the period when a series of paintings including *Solar Wind VI* was executed, Held painted exclusively in black and white, thus suggesting a deep recessive space where pure, geometric forms collide and overlap.

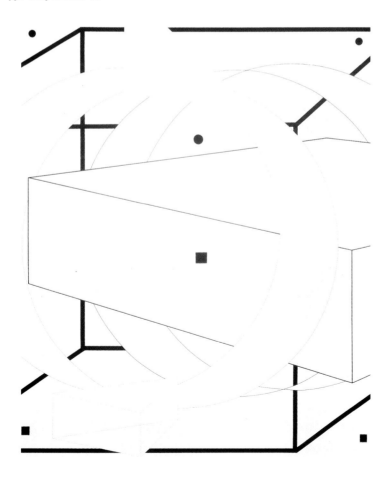

Cat. No. 88
Robert Henri (1865-1929)
Marjorie Reclining, 1918
Oil on canvas, 66 × 81 cm
1981.13

In 1902 Robert Henri was asked to teach at the New York School of Art, which had been founded in 1896 by William Merritt Chase as the Chase School of Art. A pupil of the Pennsylvania Academy of Art, and the Académie Julian in Paris, Henri's technique and teaching methods departed markedly from the long-standing tradition established by Chase, who had been the nation's foremost art teacher since 1891. Henri introduced the illustrative narrative glimpse of everyday life—or Realism—into early twentieth-century painting. His teachings and bravura manner had great impact on the new generation of painters including students Edward Hopper (Cat. Nos. 90-92) and Guy Pène du Bois (Cat. Nos. 74, 75). The civilised, distant ele-gance of Chase lost out. Calling his art vulgar, Chase broke with Henri and left to teach at the Art Students League. 1908 was a very important year for Henri. As a protest he organised an exhibition for the group The Eight—which included Ernest Lawson (Cat. No. 33)—at the Macbeth Gallery in New York. The goal of the exhibition was to challenge and break the established monopoly on exhibition activity of the National Academy of Art. That year he also married Marjorie Organ, the subject of *Marjorie Reclining*. The woman's reclining pose recalls that of Manet's *Olympia*, one of relaxed and confident intimacy. The warm colour scheme and the quick loose brush strokes are typical of Henri and the spontaneity of his approach.

Cat. No. 89
Hans Hofmann (1880-1966)
Vase, Furniture, and Books, 1935
Casein and oil on board,
76 × 55 cm
1977.89-a

Verso: *Untitled Still-Life*, 1935
Oil on board, 55 × 76 cm
1977.89-b

The recognition of Hans Hofmann as an artist came only late in his life although he was one of the principal innovators among the Abstract Expressionists and an influential teacher of two generations of artists in New York. Hofmann had studied in Paris from 1904 to 1914, and then set up two of his own very successful art schools in Munich (1915-32), and later in New York (1932-58). Hofmann made hundreds of drawings during the 1920s and 30s, but started concentrating on painting at the age of fifty-five (1935). In the 1930s the predominant style shared by American painters exploring abstraction was a loose Cubism. These influences, plus the Fauvist colours and Kandinsky's lyrical-spiritual abstractions are visible in the landscapes and still-lifes Hofmann produced in the late 30s, of which *Vase, Furniture, and Books*—and *Untitled Still-Life* painted on the verso—are examples. This is primarily a linear composition with a Cubist type still-life arrangement on a commode. The black linear grid, outlining objects and details restricts the vibrations of the bright colours. In his career, Hofmann embraced many disparate styles and manners which, to some extent, explains the relatively low esteem in which his works were held by the general public. Most people are not aware that Hofmann, in the early and mid-1940s, balanced extreme lights and darks, and poured and splattered paint before Clyfford Still and Jackson Pollock. During the 1950s his art became stylistically more uniform with great coloured rectangles pushing and pulling the eye in and out of the composition. Hofmann continued to produce masterpieces into his eighties and eventually reached the height of his creative powers. The Whitney Museum of American Art organised a travelling retrospective exhibition of Hoffman's paintings in 1957, and he was exhibited internationally during the 1960s.

Cat. No. 90
Edward Hopper (1882-1967)
Self-Portrait, c. 1904
Oil on canvas, 51.5 × 41.5 cm
1977.50

Edward Hopper was born in
Nyack, a small city along the Hudson River near New York. He was
one of the many artists who from
1900-06 attended the New York
School of Art under its founder
William Merritt Chase and later
Robert Henri (Cat. No. 88). Between 1906 and 1910, Hopper made
three extremely formative trips to
Europe visiting Paris, London,
Amsterdam, Brussels, and Madrid. Although supporting himself
as a commercial artist, which he
hated, his paintings were regularly exhibited, and one of his works,
Sailing, was included in the famous New York Armory Show of
1913 — known for setting American
painting on a new course. After an
important 1924, one man show at
the Frank K. M. Rehn Gallery in

New York, Hopper was able to
concentrate exclusively on painting. Nine years later, in 1933, he
had his first retrospective exhibition at the newly-founded Museum
of Modern Art. Before he died in
1967, Hopper had the rare honour
of four major retrospective exhibitions travelling around the United
States. He was widely recognised
both at home and abroad as the finest painter of the American Realist
tradition. His teacher Robert Henri imparted to his students an admiration for the Old Master painters Goya, Franz Hals, Rembrandt and Diego Velázquez which
accounts for the heavy paintlayer
and the dark colour scheme prevailing in the works painted prior
to his European visits. In *Self-Portrait*, the exclusion of eye contact
with the sitter emphasises the re-
served and introspective character
of the painter. In other pencil and
oil sketches of his student days,
Hopper seems to have struggled to
capture the gaze. He leaves, in this

composition, the eye area blank. In
later compositions, Hopper uses
the deliberate lack of eye contact
between the figures depicted and
the viewer as a means of creating
the isolation and big-city loneliness
which permeates the masterpieces
of his career.

Cat. No. **91**
Edward Hopper (1882-1967)
My Roof, 1928
Watercolour, 35 × 50 cm
Signed lower right:
"Edward Hopper, New York"
1977.8

Edward Hopper began painting his watercolours in 1923, and eventually became extremely successful in this medium. In 1924 Hopper married the painter Josephine Verstille Nivison. His classmate from the New York School of Art, Guy Pène du Bois (Cat. Nos. 74, 75), was his best man. Hopper's wife, nicknamed Jo, became his life-long companion, model, and the one who kept meticulous records of all his works. In volume I, page 67 of these record books, now conserved at the Whitney Museum of American Art, New York, Jo wrote about this watercolour: "3 Washington Square, North, N.Y. City. Skylight & light over hall & grey glass red tin rim." This watercolour was painted on the roof of the building where Hopper occupied two top floor adjoining studios from 1913 until death in 1967. The watercolour belongs to a series which would result in the oil painting *City Roofs*, 1932, (Private Collection) and is almost identical—although reversed—to the drypoint etching of 1915-18 *On My Roof* (Whitney Museum of American Art, New York). Hopper was fascinated by the strange "landscape" of smokestacks, chimneys, ventilator shafts and skylights; and the play of sharp light on the architectural shapes. He was among the first painters to introduce the "commercial landscape" of gas stations, motels, shops, cafeterias, offices, and movie theatres into American painting. During his long career, Hopper strove to represent, in a simplified and highly structured manner, the ordinary aspects of everyday reality in modern America, both in the big city, and in the countryside.

Cat. No. **92**
Edward Hopper (1882-1967)
Rocky Cove, 1929
Watercolour on paper,
34.2 × 49.5 cm
Signed lower right: "Edward
Hopper/Two Lights, Me."
1977.81

Edward Hopper and his wife Jo
first visited Two Lights, Cape El-
izabeth, Maine, in the summer of
1927. They returned a second time
in 1929. Boats, harbours, rivers,
and the coast had been the first
subjects Hopper explored as a
young boy. They remained vital
subjects throughout his career.
Hopper himself called his art austere, simple—even sometimes
cold, but never without richness.
He carefully selected every subject matter—in this case the large
dark rocks in the foreground "near
Maxwell's, much in silhouette," as
his wife Jo noted about *Rocky Cove*
in the book of records she kept on
her husband's work. Hopper here

uses a sombre colour scheme of
blacks, browns, dark greens, and
blues that are unusual both for the
medium (watercolour) and for the
subject (summer beach front).

Cat. No. 93
Johannes Itten (1888-1967)
Kindly Light (Gütiges Licht),
1963
Oil on canvas, 100 × 72 cm
Signed and dated on the back
of the canvas: "Itten 1963"
1964.10

"Johannes Itten. Artist and Teacher" was the title of a major retrospective exhibition at the Kunstmuseum, Bern in 1984-85. This exhibition brought out the immense importance of Johannes Itten's work as an art teacher in the development of his own creative output. Together with Paul Klee, he ranks among the most important Swiss artists of the twentieth century — internationally famous not only for his paintings, but for his achievements as a remarkably gifted teacher and art theoretician. He was born in Südern Linden of the Bernese Oberland. It was 1913, in the city of Stuttgart, however, where he made his debut as a pain-

ter. In 1916, he had already presented a one-man exhibition of primarily abstract paintings at Der Sturm Gallery in Berlin. Itten decided then for financial reasons to take up a teaching position in Vienna. Through Alma Mahler, Walter Gropius got acquainted with Itten, who had developed an interesting form and colour program for his art students. Itten was asked to join the Bauhaus in Weimar to run the preparatory course. This fascinating project which made Itten and the Bauhaus internationally known, gave him little time to paint. Works from his years at the Bauhaus (1919-23) are, therefore, rare. During these years, Klee and Kandinsky joined the teaching staff of the Bauhaus. Itten was deeply influenced by Eastern religious philosophy, particularly Zen Buddhism and Mazdaznan. At the Bauhaus, he walked around with a clean shaven head, and exercised a magical, holy fascination on his adoring pupils. Leaving the Bau-

haus for a three-year immersion in the Mazdaznan activities centred in Herrliberg, Switzerland, he subsequently, in 1926, set up the Itten School in Berlin. There he offered courses in painting, graphic design, photography, and literature. The school operated until 1934 when the Nazis closed it down. Itten then returned four years later to live in Zürich, Switzerland. There he directed the Arts and Crafts School, and the Museum of Decorative and Applied Arts. Up until 1960 he also directed the textile educational program of the Zürich Silk Industry and organised the installation of the Rietberg Museum. He lived in Zuerich until his death in 1967. The title of this composition refers to light, the light that shines through and is reflected in a colour. The large geometric painting in hues of warm and cool yellows was one of a series of works on the theme of light which Itten began after moving into a new and bright studio near the Limmat river in Zürich. *Kindly Light* was executed in 1963 and was bought by Baron Thyssen-Bornemisza directly from the artist shortly after its completion. The painting was included in the great 1964 retrospective exhibition of Itten's work, at the Kunsthaus in Zürich.

Cat. No. **94**
David Kakabadzé (1889-1952)
Untitled, 1920
Oil on cardboard, 52 × 61.5 cm
Signed and dated lower right
(in Georgian): [?] "1920"
Signed and dated on the back:
"D. Kakabadzé, Paris '20"
1983.34

David Kakabadzé was born in Kukhi, near Kutaisi, Georgia. He studied painting, mathematics, and physics at St. Petersburg University between 1910 and 1916. There, he became a friend of the painter Pavel Filonov. During the years 1920-27 Kakabadzé travelled extensively in Europe, yet keeping up his primary base in Paris. In 1918-19 he played a major role in the development of the Georgian Avant-Garde in Tiflis (Tbilisi). Kakabadzé returned permanently to Georgia in 1927 and lived in the capital Tbilisi until his death in 1952. A member of the Association of Artists of Revolutionary Geor-

gia, and from 1929 until 1948 a teacher at the Academy of Arts in Tbilisi, Kakabadzé adjusted his experimental style to the more repertorial and Realist demands of the time. His work of the 1930s-40s is devoted primarily to local landscapes and industrial scenes. The paintings of the Paris years are the most important in his brief but refined career. They are rare, and practically never included in exhibitions of Avant-Garde art. *Untitled* was, according to an inscription on the back, painted in Paris in 1920, shortly after Kakabadzé had settled there. This flattened urban landscape in muted military greens is set within a painted oval. All the buildings are tilted. The unsettling effect of the destabilised architectural parts is offset by balancing the different "weight" of volumes and colours, and the overall contours of the mass of buildings which contain the "falling" houses. The graphic quality of the painting is reinforced by the trun-

cated French words of Dubon-[net], Caf[é] and Hote[l]. The resulting image combines the looks of the Dada collage technique and the fragmentation of later Cubism.

Cat. No. **95**
Lajos Kassák (1887-1967)
Untitled, 1921
India ink on paper, 29 × 23 cm
Signed and dated lower left:
"Kassák 1921 Wien"
Signed upper right: "Kassák"
(upside down)
1978.65

Hungarian artist Lajos Kassák was a leader of the East and Central European Constructivist movement in both Budapest and Vienna. Kassák was born in poverty and always had great financial difficulties. He was an uncompromising idealist who identified with the workers and, throughout his life, persistently struggled to further social democracy and higher standards of art, literature, and poetry of the common man. His art was ignored—or at least underrated—in his native country during his lifetime. His artistic career was one of solitary perseverance and oppression. In a society shift-

ing to a radically socialist one, abstract art became a symbol of a revolutionary attitude. Philosophically, intellectually, and artistically, the publications he founded, edited, and wrote for in Budapest and later Vienna—*Tett* (Action), *Ma* (Today), and *Documentum* (Document)—exposed the Avant-Garde ideology reflected in Wassily Kandinsky's and Kazimir Malevich's writings of that same period. Kassák published articles by many of the most talented European artists and writers including Apollinaire, Jean Cocteau, George Bernard Shaw and Tristan Tzara, and reproductions of works by Alexander Archipenko, Hans Arp, Marc Chagall, Umberto Boccioni, André Derain, Kandinsky, Fernand Léger, Max Pechstein, and Kurt Schwitters among others. *Tett* was banned in 1915 because it published anti-war articles. *Ma* was further banned in 1919 because Kassák in an open letter to Béla Kun, the leader of the regime, wrote against

the curbing of free speech and censorship of art and literature introduced by the socialists. Kassák was imprisoned for his outspoken non-conformist views, but he managed to flee to Vienna in 1920. From there he continued the publishing of *Ma*. This journal covered all the arts including the second generation of German Expressionists, and Surrealism but extended distinctly towards Russian Constructivism. Kassák's work can be divided into two phases, separated by twenty years: the first during the late teens and the twenties, and the second from the end of World War II until his death in 1967. It was during the years of his exile in Vienna (1920-26) that Kassák produced his most interesting work. Whereas he had written poetry and articles for many years, he now took up painting. Typography with its visual structuring of shape, size, and arrangement of letters and lines fascinated him. They led him to develop his own style of collage and commercial art. Kassák's ink drawings and gouaches of the early 1920s, of which *Untitled* is an example, bear a striking resemblance to the Suprematist works of Kliun, Popova, and Rodchenko. They are composed of primary geometric forms such as circles, squares, rectangles, lines, and triangles which aim at representing order, logic, rationality, and organisation. Kassák called these geometric compositions of the 1920s "Bildarchitektur." The present composition is a study in india ink for No. 7 of a set of seven lithographs included in the "Ma" series of 1921, and all seven lithographs are variations of geometric abstractions in black on white. Kassák returned to Hungary in the 1930s when a general amnesty made it possible. He had to give up painting, however, because the cultural policy, or rather intolerance of the regime repressed Avant-Garde art. In the mid-1960s the political oppression eased and he was allowed to exhibit it in the West. Although he wasn't permitted to leave Hungary to attend a 1962 major exhibition of his works in Paris. Kassák was pleased to finally achieve international recognition—an appreciation he received in his own country only after his death.

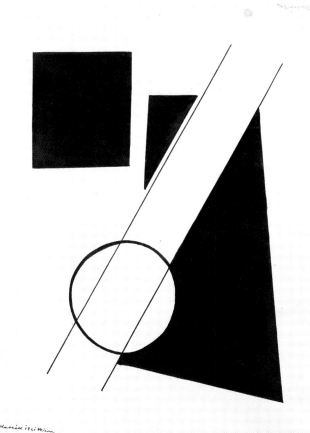

Cat. No. **96**
Lee Krasner (1912-1984)
Red, White, Blue, Yellow, Black,
1939
Oil on paper with collage,
63 × 48 cm
Signed with initials and dated
right of lower centre: "L.K. '39"
1978.9

When Lee Krasner enrolled at the
New York Hans Hofmann School
of Fine Arts in 1937, she had already studied for over seven years
at other art schools and worked for
the Public Works of Art Project.
Hofmann's teachings were inspiring, and helped foster the talented
student's experimentation with
abstraction and collage. She was
still at Hofmann's school when she
painted *Red, White, Blue, Yellow,
Black* which demonstrates her
precocious and original treatment
of both colour and shape. At Hofmann's school, still-lifes of objects,
including the one Hofmann depicts
in *Vase, Furniture, and Books,*

and *Untitled Still-Life* painted on
the verso (1935) (Cat. No. 89 a-b),
became Krasner's point of departure for this abstract composition
in five primary colours. The artist
used her own discarded works for a
collage type of composition; cutting and pasting sections of old
paintings into a new and dynamic
context. Krasner has a firm position within the first generation of
Abstract Expressionists in America. She was married to Jackson
Pollock (Cat. Nos. 126-128), and a
close friend of among others Alfonso Ossorio (Cat. No. 122). During
the 1970s, Krasner again took out
drawings and paintings which had
been inspired by Picasso and done
while still a student of Hofmann.
Cutting, pasting and incorporating
sections of these forty years worth
of old Cubist studies, Krasner created an outstanding series of abstract compositions.

Cat. No. 97
Walt Kuhn (1877-1949)
Chorus Captain, 1935
Oil on canvas, 102 × 76.2 cm
Signed and dated lower right:
" Walt Kuhn 1935"
1979.35

William (Walt) Kuhn was born in Brooklyn, New York, in 1877. His earliest professional activity was owning a bicycle shop. By 1899, he had started a career as a cartoonist in Los Angeles. This career led to a two-year stay in Paris and Munich from 1901 to 1902. Kuhn worked primarily as a cartoonist for several New York based papers and magazines during the years 1905-14. Shortly after his first one-man show at the Madison Gallery, New York (1910-11), Walt Kuhn became one of the organisers—the Executive Secretary—of the famous New York Armory Show, which, in 1913, brought the latest European and American art together. Henri Matisse, Paul Cézanne, Pablo Picasso, and Marcel Duchamp, just to mention a few, caused a sensation and left lasting impressions on a generation of artists who were to change the course of American painting. Throughout the 1920s, Kuhn was involved with theatrical reviews in New York and Chicago. During the summer of 1922, Kuhn had worked for the Earl Carrol Theatre's (New York) performance of Michio Ito's *Pinwheel Revue*, taking a particular interest in clowns and dancers. He was to use these models repeatedly throughout the 1920s, 30s and 40s. *Chorus Captain* shows a glamorous female dancer off-stage. Traditionally, the chorus captain is the most stunning of the dancers in the chorus line of musicals. Heavily made up and dressed in a huge pink ostrich head dress and pink bandeau, the young girl absent-mindedly stares out in front of her. Kuhn follows the tradition of Watteau and Picasso in depicting the sad clown or performer who lacks the broad smile and self-confident posture which is usually associated with entertainers.

Cat. No. 98
Mikhail Fedorovich Larionov
(1881-1964)
The Quarrel (La Rixe), 1911
Oil on canvas, 71.3 × 94 cm
Signed on verso:
"Larionoff La rixe."
1987.17

Mikhail Fedorovich Larionov is one of the original inventors of non-objective art. He enrolled at the Moscow Institute of Painting, Sculpture, and Architecture in 1898. There he met Natalia Goncharova in 1900 and became her life-long companion. Some of the richest and most interesting experiments of Avant-Garde painting created during the crucial years of the first two decades of the twentieth century were by these two artists. They began by introducing elements of traditional Russian folk art into the so-called Neo-Primitive paintings of around 1907. They went on to explore the abstract potential of Cubism and Futurism, an experiment which led to the development of Rayonism in 1912, which is one of the earliest non-representational styles of painting. Larionov exhibited at the Salon d'Automne in Paris in 1906 and coorganised important Avant-Garde exhibitions in Moscow and St. Petersburg such as "Jack of Diamonds," "Donkey's Tail," "Target," and "No. 4," until he was mobilised in 1914. When he was wounded in action in 1915 and demobilised, he joined Diaghilev, then residing in Lausanne. Their cooperation on the Ballets Russes continued in Paris through 1929. He settled with Goncharova in Paris in 1917, and remained there until his death. The artist couple exhibited together at the Kingore Gallery in New York in 1922, and at the Shiseido Gallery in Tokyo in 1923, but then fell into comparative obscurity. Except for occasional contributions to exhibitions, Larionov lived unrecognised and impoverished from 1930 onward, and his position as one of the great innovators of modern art was only appreciated after his death. *The Quarrel* is one of several amusing scenes from Larionov's military service in 1910-11, and painted shortly thereafter. The painting with its bold execution, and expressive crudeness of figures set in a naïve tilted space belongs to Larionov's Neo-Primitivist period.

Cat. No. **99**
Vladimir Vasilievich Lebedev
(1891-1967)
Cubism: Portrait (Kubismus),
c. 1920
Oil on canvas, 85 × 68 cm
Signed with initials in Russian
lower right: "VL."
1983.35a-b

Alongside the more famous of the
artists who during the first two
decades of the twentieth century,
formed the Russian Avant-Garde
Vladimir Vasilievich Lebedev occupied a less well-known position.
Lebedev lived and worked in St.
Petersburg where he studied at
the Academy of Arts (1912-18), and
was Professor of the Academy
from 1918 to 1921. His main documented activity was heading the
Petrograd/Leningrad branch of
the "ROSTA" which, over a period
of two years (1920-22) produced
around six hundred high quality
propaganda posters. An important
part of these posters were illustrated in the 1923 book published
by Punin, *The Russian Poster
1917-22.* Lebedev participated in
the preparations for the five-year
jubilee of the Russian Revolution
and subsequently directed a children's book publishing house for
which he also produced illustrations. The composition from the
important period in his life *Cubism: Portrait* represents a clever
synthesis of Cubist and Suprematist stylistic features. The circles,
rectangles, and squares in black,
white, red, and grey are characteristic of Suprematism and have
been combined with the faceting
and blurring of the separation between the typically Cubist motif
and the environment. Because of
the strong element of Suprematism, the resulting portrait stands
quite apart from French, other
Western European, and American
Cubist tendencies of the time. It
remains firmly rooted in the Russian painting of the late 1910s and
1920s.

Cat. No. 100
Fernand Léger (1881-1955)
Man and Woman, 1921
Watercolour, 36.5 × 26.5 cm
Signed and dated lower right:
"FL 21"
1976.94

Man and Woman was executed during Fernand Léger's so called "mechanical" period. This period began with his return from army service after the World War I, and lasted until 1924. Léger trained as an architect, and was never formally admitted at the Ecole des Beaux-Arts, had exhibited at D.H. Kahnweiler's Gallery in Paris with the Cubists Pablo Picasso and Georges Braque from 1910 until 1914. During that same period, he befriended Robert Delaunay, experimented with colour and abstraction, and given lectures at the Académie Vassilieff. From the Pre-War isolation of the painter's studio, Léger suddenly found himself "on a level with the whole of the

French people. My new companions in the Engineer Corps were miners, navvies, workers in metal and wood. Among them I discovered the French people. At the same time I was dazzled by the breech of a 75-millimetre gun which was standing uncovered in the sunlight: the magic of light on white metal. This was enough to make me forget the abstract art of 1912-13. A complete revelation to me, both as a man and as a painter." In *Man and Woman*, a few primary colours illuminate the modulated hues of grey which confirm body to rounded shapes of neck, arms, and hip. Léger's colours are applied to flat areas and create a sense of movement and dynamic tension. Léger reduces forms to simple, geometric shapes in a balanced order around black and white. Long before the American Pop artists, Léger took to the bold designs and bright colours of posters, advertisements, commercial packaging, and machines. He

also created a certain type of man: the construction worker. In his admiration for robots and machines, Léger's figures are mostly grey and featureless, frontal and immobile. In this sense, Léger shares ideas with the Russian Avant-Garde, particularly Kazimir Malevich (Cat. No. 103). When *Man and Woman* was painted, Léger was working on illustrations for the André Malraux book *Paper Moons* and the stage sets for the Swedish ballet *The Skating Rink*. The Futurists, Suprematists and Constructivists, as well as the Dadaists, and American Precisionists shared the admiration for the machine and its promise of a bright new world. He first visited the United States in 1931 and he then settled in New York between 1940-45, where he became more popular than he had been in Europe. When returning to France in 1945, Léger, received a large number of official commissions and honours.

Cat. No. **101**
Richard Lindner (1901-1978)
Out of Towners, 1968
Pencil and red ink on paper,
60 × 50 cm
Signed lower right:
"R. Lindner 1968"
1973.27

The German-born Richard Lindner was almost fifty years old before he decided to give up a brilliant career as an illustrator and become a full-time painter. Of Jewish descent, Lindner had fled Germany when the Nazis came to power in 1933. He settled in Paris from where he emigrated to the United States in 1941. Lindner was a big city person, and called himself a New Yorker, not an American. He concentrated on the depiction of people, animals, and objects. A colourful and provocative exhibitionism ties Lindner's world view in with the German Neue Sachlichkeit artists like Fernand Léger (Cat. No. 100) and Giorgio de Chirico (Cat. Nos. 64, 65), who were influential on his construction of the human figure, and his dream-like, box-like picture space. Lindner's art does not fit into any specific artistic movement, although he is often classified as a Pop artist. He said himself that, like his good friend Saül Steinberg (Cat. No. 144), he painted the impressions of a European tourist who arrives in New York and sees everything in a different manner from a native American. *Out of Towners*, of 1968, is one of a series of of New York views called "Fun City." The Statue of Liberty, symbol of New York sightseeing, is the backdrop of the depiction of a grotesque couple: the Out of Towners. In Lindner's work, the woman is always dominating and aggressive, enhancing her appearance with provocative make-up and a wealth of colourful accessories.

Cat. No. **102**
August Macke (1887-1914)
Flowers, c. 1913
Watercolour, india and coloured
inks on paper, 28.5 × 23.5 cm
1969.9

August Macke was born in Mes-
chede, Westfälen (the Ruhr dis-
trict), but spent the first thirteen
years of his life in Cologne. Driven
by an intense and all-absorbing interest in drawing, he went—
against his father's wishes—to
Düsseldorf to study at the Academy and remained there until 1905.
This was a period when young German painters felt that they were
living in the centre of Europe, that
Cologne and Bonn were like sur-
burbs of Paris, Rome and Vienna, and that their main education
consisted in travelling a lot to see
contemporary art all over Europe. During the years 1905 to 1910
Macke visited Italy, Holland,
Belgium, London and Paris several times. The turning point in
Macke's early artistic formation
was his encounter with the Impressionists Georges Seurat and
Edgar Degas in Paris. In a letter to
his future bride Elisabeth Ger-
hardt, he wrote how the discovery
of these paintings made him feel
that he had come out of the dark-
ness and into the sunlight. These
trips gave Macke new inspiration
for his drawings, watercolours,
and oil paintings. He had been an
intimate friend of Franz Marc
(Cat. No. 107), ever since the two
met in Marc's Munich studio in
1910—the year Macke and his new
bride settled in a house on the Te-
gernsee not far from Munich. As
soulmates, they shared a profound
interest in the new theories of
Wassily Kandinsky, and they both
joined Kandinsky's newly-formed
Blaue Reiter (Blue Rider) group.
They participated in publication of
the *Blaue Reiter Almanach* which
was edited by Kandinsky and Ga-
briele Münter, both then residing
in Murnau outside of Munich.
When Macke met Sonia and Robert Delaunay in 1912 on a trip to Paris accompanied by Marc, and subsequently in his own home the following year, his treatment of colour changed under the influence of
Robert Delaunay's prismatic colour theories. In 1912, Macke participated in and organised several
exhibitions such as the "Blaue Reiter" exhibition Munich (1912),
"Sonderbund" exhibition, Cologne

(1912), "Rheinische Expressionis-
ten," Bonn (1913), and the "Erste
Deutscher Herbstsalon" in Berlin,
(1913). All five works by Macke in
the Thyssen-Bornemisza Collection, of which *Flowers* is one, date
from 1913 and 1914—the last years
of Macke's life. From the summer
of 1913 to June 1914, Macke and his
family lived in the Haus Rosengar-
ten right on Lake Thun in Hilter-
fingen, Switzerland. During this
period, Macke created some of his
most important mature works. He
had also been working on sketches
for plates, glasses, and embroider-
ies in 1912. It is possible that this
little watercolour of stylised trees
or flowers was intended for a fabric
design. In 1914 Macke met Paul
Klee and, together with Louis
Moilliet, the three artists planned
a spring journey to Tunis which
was to become a revolutionary
trip. During this trip, colour took
on an autonomous life, and works
produced upon return from this
stay became the culmination of

Macke's life's work. His short, but
brilliant career was brutally cut
when he was killed in action, in
September 1914, after serving a
month and a half as Lieutenant of
the 160th Rhenisch Infantry Re-
giment of the German army.

Cat. No. 103
Kazimir Severinovich Malevich
(1878-1935)
Untitled, c. 1919
Gouache on paper, 31.7 × 23.8 cm
1980.53

Kazimir Severinovich Malevich was a predominant figure of the Russian Avant-Garde movement from around 1910 to 1930. Before developing the system of abstract painting called "Suprematism" in 1915, Malevich had moved through a range of styles from Impressionism and Post-Impressionism, into Neo-Primitivism, Cubism and Cubo-Futurism. In simple terms Suprematism is an artistic language composed solely of geometrical shapes with no reference to the visible world of man and nature; it is practically free of all naturalistic and traditional connotations. At the watershed "Last Futurist Exhibition. 0.10" in St. Petersburg in 1915-16, Malevich showed the painting *Black Square*—his first

entirely non-objective composition. *Black Square* was hung as an icon across the upper corner of the exhibition room, and exemplified the artist's concept of the "Zero-form" of painting. Other abstract art, revolutionary as it was at the time, originated in some sort of vision, or an object and was therefore linked to the representation of an aspect of reality. Malevich's work and theories about painting, however, were among the first examples of a painterly system rejecting the object and the representational, reducing form and colour to the minimum. The artist exposed his ideas in the publication *From Cubism and Futurism to Suprematism* which accompanied the "0.10" exhibition. Along with many of the remarkable Russian artists of the Avant-Garde including Marc Chagall, Ilia Chashnik (Cat. Nos. 62, 63), Natalia Gontcharova, Wassily Kandinsky, Mikhail Larionov (Cat. No. 98) and El Lissitzky, Malevich enthusiasti-

cally participated in the first formation of art and design schools in the new Russia after the Revolution of October, 1917. Malevich, who was also a brilliant teacher, was asked by Chagall to teach at the Vitebsk Art Practical Institute, and subsequently took over the directorship of the school from Chagall from 1919 to 1922. In Vitebsk Malevich taught Suprematism and headed the group Unovis (Affirmers of the New Art) which consisted of a handful of his students at the school including Chashnik, El Lissitzky and Nikolai Suetin. *Untitled* is an example of the theories of Suprematism exemplified in Malevich's works following the famous "0.10" exhibition. The background of the paper creates the sensation of infinity of space on which monochrome, geometric shapes flow, collide, converge, or recede. *Untitled* includes four rectangles: one central, black, placed horizontally; and three smaller and slimmer, placed vertically, with red in the centre. The careful balance of few primary colours and simple geometric shapes is characteristic of Suprematism. Suprematist works by Malevich were, no doubt, imbued with theosophic and mystic thoughts, but works by many other artists working in the Suprematist mode easily turned into pure decoration. In his last years Malevich returned to figurative painting. At the end of the 1920s, the idealism of the first Post-Revolution years was replaced by an obligation to suppress useless personal artistic expression in favour of a streamlined system of utilitarian conformist objects for the masses. The artists who had initially been celebrated as creative forces in the new society were now sometimes seen as dangerous marginals, and the best, including Malevich, either retired from public life or were persecuted as formalists. Malevich had exhibited in Berlin at the "First Russian Exhibition" in 1922, and he travelled to Warsaw and again to Berlin for his first one-man show in 1927. A large corpus of his paintings from this exhibition was entrusted for safekeeping to a friend. These surfaced after the War, when very little of Malevich's work was known outside the USSR, and gave us an important insight into the creative process of this great artist.

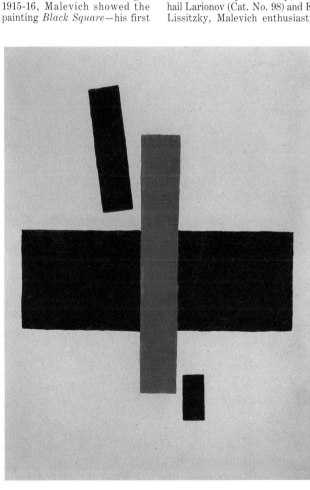

Cat. No. 104
Paul Mansouroff
(Pavel Andreevich Mansurov)
(1896-1984)
Painterly Formula
(Formule Picturale) c. 1918
Oil on panel, 133 × 26.9 cm
Signed in Russian and dated
lower right centre:
"P. Mansouroff 1918."
1977.114

While a young student at the Stieglitz Institute of Painting in St. Petersburg (1909-14), Paul Mansouroff achieved, independently of other artists, compositions bordering on abstraction of nature studies. During service in the Imperial Airforce from 1915-17, he worked on technical drawings of aeronautic and military equipment, thus requiring a high degree of precision and refined line. This was to characterise his later work. From 1917 onward, Mansouroff established a strongly defined personal position in the development of non-figurative art and Constructivism. He came in close contact with Pavel Filonov, Kazimir Malevich (Cat. No. 103), Mikhail Matiushin, Ivan Puni, and Vladimir Tatlin. Together they formed the "State Institute of Artistic Culture" (Ginkhuk) which was established at the Miatlev Palace, Petrograd, in 1922. Until Mansouroff left Russia in 1928 for Italy, and subsequently Paris, he headed the Experimental Section of the Ginkhuk. In Paris Mansouroff obtained work from fashion houses for haute couture textile designs. Like many other Russian emigré artists, Mansouroff lived and worked in France as a recluse. He died in Nice in 1984, as the last of the great Russian Avant-Garde painters, faithful to his original principles until the end. Mansouroff applied the format and title of *Painterly Formula* to a number of important abstract compositions from this period. He used old rough boards or wooden planks, and painted on these uneven structures. He chose a limited range of colours, with a predominance of the grey scale. The wooden support has a natural sculptural effect, and the verticality of the composition is further emphasised by the long thin and imperceptively curved lines in white, red and black floating on a grey background and framed by a colour field of green and white on either side.

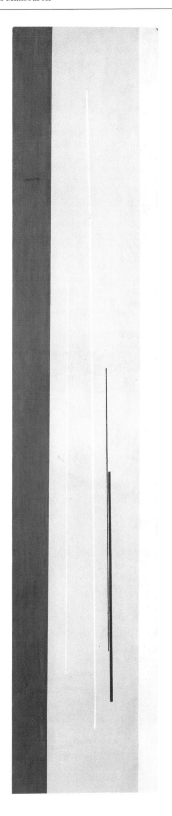

Cat. No. **105**
Paul Mansouroff
(Pavel Andreevich Mansurov)
(1896-1984)
Untitled, c. 1923-24
Oil on panel, 127 × 40.8 cm
Signed in cyrillic lower centre:
"P Mansouroff"
1983.5

Paul Mansouroff said that "the
only kind of genuine art is one that
does not repeat previous trends,
one that does not make inferences
on the basis of preceding models."
His own work is an illustration of
this idea and belongs to the category of artistic expression in which
a unique, artistic language was invented. Painted on a roughly hewn
and slightly curved wooden plank,
Untitled is an example of Mansouroff's remarkable abstract compositions of the mid-1920s. This was
the time when he was heading the
Experimental Section of the Ginkhuk in Petrograd and was in close
contact with the primary artists
and critics of the Avant-Garde:
Pavel Filonov, Kazimir Malevich
(Cat. No. 103), Mikhail Matiushin,
Ivan Puni, and Vladimir Tatlin.
The volumetric forms floating on
subtlely and precisely modeled
planes of white, grey, and black repeat the shape of the wooden support. Whereas the tinge of yellow
backlights the upper outlines of
the triangular forms and adds
three-dimensionality to the composition. Mansouroff had a successful exhibition in Rome in 1928.
In spite of his prominent position
in the development of non-objective art there were no other one-
man exhibitions of his paintings for
over thirty years; that is, until his
work was rediscovered in the
1960s. For years, he refused to
part with his paintings of the late
teens and twenties including such
works as *Painterly Formula* and
Untitled, which are remarkable
individualistic contributions to
Russian Avant-Garde art. In
these works, Mansouroff strives to
achieve "an absolute clarity dictated by the inner idea...in-
finity..."emptiness." Mansouroff
achieved international recognition
when the Musée d'Art Moderne in
Paris gave him a major retrospective in 1972.

Cat. No. **106**
Man Ray (1890-1976)
Keyhole (Trou de Serrure), 1928
Oil on canvas, 45.5 × 38 cm
Signed and dated lower right:
"Man Ray 1928"
1979.16

New York Dada owed its stimulus
to the 1915 arrival from Europe of
Francis Picabia (Cat. No. 125) and
Marcel Duchamp. They were flee-
ing from France during World War
I and ultimately joined the American Man Ray. An artist of tremendous inventiveness in the making
of objects and creating new techniques, Man Ray was the only native American among the New
York Dadaists. The Dada movement in New York disintegrated in
1921 when Man Ray departed for
Paris. Except for the years 1940-
51, in which the artist spent his
time in the United States, Man
Ray lived permanently in Paris. In
Paris Dada emerged as Surrealism
in 1925, although their principles
were somewhat different—Surrealism aims at expressing the lib-
erated, unconscious activity of the
mind and represents an exploration into the unknown. Surrealism
is a journey into the interior as an
illustration of a thought or perception. It often exalts eros as act and
instinct. *Keyhole* was painted in
Paris in the heyday of the Surrealist movement. The irresistible, almost magic attraction of the keyhole is evident: An eye—often
used in Surrealist imagery—peep-
ing through the keyhole, is pre-
sumably spying on some kind of
erotic act.

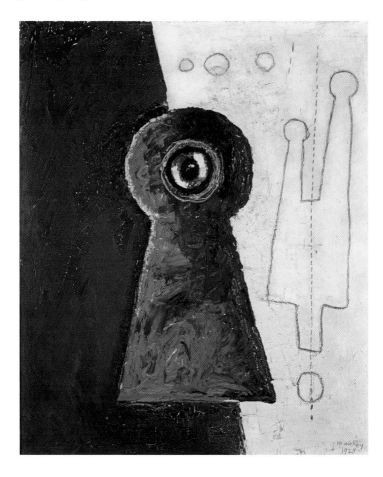

Cat. No. **107**
Franz Marc (1880-1916)
*Goblet with Fox and Deer
(Pokal mit Fuchs und Rehbock),*
1915
Mixed media art collage,
15.7 × 12.2 cm
Signed and inscribed upper
centre: "Alfred Mayer kredenzt
im Kriegsjahr 1915 von f.m."
1975.32

Franz Marc was one of the many
young talented German artists
who served in the World War I; he
was killed in action in 1916. According
to his widow Maria Marc, *Goblet with Fox and Deer* was the only
watercolour executed by the artist
while in the German Army. This
accounts for its importance in his
oeuvre. This little card, filled with
not readily intelligible symbolic
references was, as it is inscribed,
made for his friend, supporter, and
patron Alfred Mayer. He had visited Mayer while on leave from the
Army during July or November of
1915. The rather unusual object depicted could be either a goblet, a
tankard, or perhaps even a baptismal font carved with mythical animals, of which a fox and a deer can
vaguely be identified. The execution also includes the affixing of silver foil, suggesting perhaps the
guilding of ancient sacramental objects. Marc has been called "an animal painter" and it is true that he
concentrated a great part of his
creative energy on the depiction
of animals as symbols of primitive but genuine spirituality and
strength. A profound religious
faith and interest in biblical subjects remained vital to his outlook
on life and is reflected in his creative output. Franz Marc was born
in Munich in 1880. His father was a
painter, and Franz initially studied
theology and philosophy before deciding to study painting in 1900.
During visits to Paris in 1903 and
1907, the Impressionists and Vincent van Gogh made a strong impact on his technique. Marc was
one of the artists participating in
the "Neue Künstlervereinigung
München," and in the formation
and first exhibitions of the Blaue
Reiter group in 1911. Among his
closest friends were August Macke
(Cat. No. 102) and Wassily Kandinsky whom he had met in Munich in
1910. In 1912, he returned with
Macke to Paris. There he met Robert Delaunay who was to have a
great influence on his treatment of
colour. That same year, an exhibition of Futurism at the Der Sturm
Gallery in Berlin also left noticeable traces on his production.
From 1913 he worked on Bible illustrations exploring an idea he
had developed with Kandinsky,
Paul Klee, Alfred Kubin, and Oskar Kokoschka. While in the Army
he continued working on these Bible illustrations, and on sketches
from the field. *Goblet with Fox and
Deer* is the last watercolour painted by this remarkable artist.

Cat. No. **108**
John Marin (1870-1953)
New York Series, 1927
Watercolour and tempera
on paper, 67 × 54 cm
Signed and dated lower right:
"Marin 27"
1981.9

John Marin spent the formative
years of his artistic training from
1905 to 1910 in Paris, at the time
when Pablo Picasso's first Cubist
compositions such as *Les Demoiselles d'Avignon*, 1907 (Museum of
Modern Art, New York), were
propelling figurative art into that
gradual dissolution of the object
which was to become one of the epoch-breaking innovations in twentieth-century art. Already by 1909
Marin's work was promoted by the
avant-garde gallery owner Alfred
Stieglitz at his Photo-Secession
Gallery on 291 Fifth Avenue. Marin's Cubism was poetic and decorative, rather than a cerebral exer-
cise in shaping the seen according
to a set of rules. In a continuing series of views of New York, especially Lower Manhattan—executed between 1910 his return to the
States and 1953 (his death)—Marin
focused on the city with skyscrapers as the dominant feature. Initially, Marin had trained as an architect, and his interest in architectural forms pervaded his city
views. *New York Series* of 1927 is
one of many such views from the
late 1920s—a critical decade for
Marin. The frame-within-a-frame
is a distinct feature of Marin's compositions of this period.

Cat. No. **109**
John Marin (1870-1953)
Eastport, Maine, 1933
Watercolour on paper,
43 × 33.6 cm
Signed and dated lower right:
"Marin 33"
1979.70

John Marin spent his first summer on the coast of Maine in 1914 and, over the years, continued to return. In 1933 he purchased a house at Cape Split near Addison, Maine, and spent his summers there. New York was Marin's first focus but the coastal views of Maine became another major theme his work. Line was essential for Marin. "Drawing and paint side by side make for the Splendid," Marin said about the technique he employed in such semi-abstract compositions as *Eastport, Maine*. A green sailboat framed by dynamic black lines is executed over a Cubist-inspired grid; the sailboat is recognisable, but submerged into the pattern of black calligraphic lines and fluid colour fields. Throughout the thirties, Marin continued to explore the vitality of landscapes and seascapes, and also started working more with figural compositions and oils. In 1936, Marin was honoured by a major retrospective exhibition of his work at the Museum of Modern Art, New York. He continued to work until his death at the age of eighty-three.

Cat. No. **110**
Marino Marini (1901-1980)
Rider on a Red Horse, 1952
Indian ink and tempera on paper,
60 × 39 cm
Signed and dated lower right:
"Marino Marini '52"
1963.4

Marino Marini is one of the most
important sculptors of our century. He was born in Pistoia, Italy, in
1901. Marini enrolled at the Accademia di Belle Arti in Florence in
1917, and initially studied painting.
From 1922 onward, sculpture became an increasingly important aspect of his work. Marini participated in the "Second Biennale" in
Rome in 1923 and, at the termina-
tion of his studies at the Academy
that same year, he set up his first
studio in Florence. In 1929 Marini
moved to Milan. Sculpture was by
now his main interest, representing primarily horses, nudes, and
portraits. Abroad, Marini first exhibited in Nice (1929), and the fol-

lowing years in Bern, Basel, and
Stockholm. He had his first one-
man show at the Galleria Milano in
1932. At the Second "Quadrien-
nale" (1935) in Rome, Marini won
the prize for sculpture and was recognised as one of the most original
sculptors of Italy. The following
year Marini travelled extensively
through Germany and Greece and
ultimately returned to Paris,
which he had previously visited in
1928, 1930, and 1931. In 1938 he
married Mercedes Pedrazzini (Ma-
rina) from Tenero-Locarno, Ticino. Marini taught sculpture at the
Accademia di Brera, Milan from
1940 but, when his studio was
bombed the following year, he
moved to the house of his inlaws in
Switzerland where he stayed until
1946. In his first one-man show at
Curt Valentine Gallery in New
York in 1950, the images and sculptures of horse and rider brought
Marini instant international fame.
Marini's horses are not traditional
symbols of power and triumph but

expressions of tragedy, agony, and
catastrophe caused by World War
II. Over the years, Marini's horses
became increasingly disturbed and
agitated, and the riders increasingly incapable of domineering the
animals. Marino's preparatory
drawings and watercolours for
sculptures are important records
of his first "ideas." *Rider on a Red
Horse* of 1952 is related to a number of bronzes from the 1950s
where the horse appears fright-
ened and the rider—as in the position here depicted—throws his
arms up in the air in a gesture of
horror.

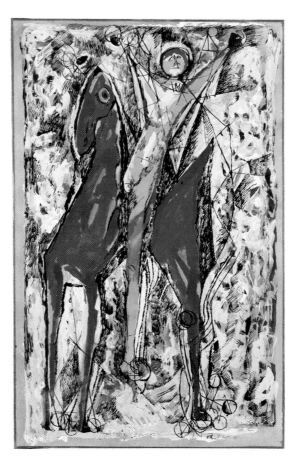

Cat. No. 111
Reginald Marsh (1898-1954)
*Food Store (The Death
of Dillinger)*, 1938
Tempera 71.1 × 50.8 cm
Signed and dated lower right:
"REGINALD MARSH '38"
1978.24

Reginald Marsh was born the son
of American painters studying in
Paris. Like many American artists, Marsh began working as a
New York illustrator drawing city
subjects and theatrical sketches.
From 1925 he worked notably for
the *New Yorker, Esquire, Fortune*
and *Life* magazines which he continued doing for many years.
Marsh belonged to the group of
painters who, like Guy Pène du
Bois (Cat. Nos. 74, 75) concentrated on the American urban scene,
with a strong narrative emphasis
originating in illustrative report-
ing. *Food Store (The Death of Dillinger)* is in fact a version of an illustration for an article in the

March 11, 1940, issue of *Life* magazine, depicting the 1934 dramatic
killing of the Chicago gangster,
John Dillinger. Dillinger, who had
long been wanted by the police,
was framed outside a movie-theat-
re by two women—one of whom
was wearing a bright red dress—
and shot to death by FBI gunmen.

Cat. No. **112**
André Masson (1896-1987)
The Statue (La Statue) 1925
Oil on canvas, 55 × 33 cm
Signed on verso: "André Masson"
1975.17

André Masson was a child prodigy and only nine years old when he was accepted as a student at at L'Académie Royale des Beaux Arts in Brussels. As an artist he came in contact with Cubism in 1919, shortly after being released from war service in the French Army. His first Cubist-inspired still-lifes and compositions relating to *The Statue* were created in the years 1922-24, where he had an atelier adjoining that of Joan Miró on 45 Rue Blomet, Paris. He had his first one-man show at Kahnweiler's Galerie Simon, Paris in 1924. That same year, he became a close friend of the theoretician behind the Surrealist group which then was forming: André Breton. Masson participated in the first

Surrealist group exhibition in 1925 with Giorgio de Chirico (Cat. Nos. 64, 65), Max Ernst (Cat. Nos. 78-80), Miró, Pablo Picasso, and Man Ray (Cat. No. 106). Initially, Surrealism distinguished itself from Dada and other avant-garde movements by its cultivation of automatism, and Masson was, with Miró, among the first painters to develop this method into a very personal and distinctive style. In automatic writing, Masson lets his pen move over the paper according to its own "inner rhythm," creating symbolic imageries of fruit, birds, fish, women's breasts and hands. The method worked very well in drawing and Masson subsequently explored ways of transferring this spontaneity to oil painting, squeezing the paint out directly on the canvas, and later applying glue, sand, lines, and colour pools, in which he would discern and strengthen certain images — usually derived from mythology or violent memories of the war. Masson

took refuge during World War II in the United States where he lived and painted from 1941-47. Masson's revolutionary technique preceded Jackson Pollock's drip paintings (Cat. Nos. 126-128), and was a major influence on the development of Abstract Expressionism in America.

Cat. No. **113**
Otto Mueller (1874-1930)
Nude by a Woodland Pool
(Mädchenakt am Waldteich),
c. 1920-22
Watercolour and crayon
on paper, 50 × 34 cm
Signed lower right:
"Otto Mueller"
1974.56

The summer outings along the North and Baltic Sea coasts and the wooded areas of Bavaria and Bohemia were the most productive times of German Expressionist painters, mainly those belonging to the Die Brücke group. Also independent painters working in the Expressionist mode—which became the dominating avant-garde art form in Germany during the first three decades of the twentieth century—benefitted from these trips. German Expressionist painting abounds with nude females frolicking in the greenery. A nude in nature was—after all—

"natural." This is a theme rarely seen in American painting of the same time. Usually the models are very young girls, joining the painters for weeklong sketching trips. The paintings are not morally offensive, although the life style alluded to did cause dismay. Anatomic detail, like all detail in Expressionist painting, is summarily executed with vigour and freshness in a creative frenzy. Otto Mueller, originally from Liebau, Breslau, had studied for a short time in 1898 with the symbolist Franz von Stuck in Munich—the same year Emil Nolde (Cat. Nos. 117-121) had been refused admission to the Munich Academy. Mueller moved to Berlin in 1908. When his paintings were rejected by the Berliner Sezession in 1910 he joined Die Brücke and remained associated with the group until it was dissolved in 1913. He was particularly close to Erich Heckel, Karl Schmidt-Rottluff (Cat. No. 137), and Ernst Ludwig Kirchner.

It was Kirchner who encouraged him to adopt the fast, angular, and sketchy method characterising his works from 1910 onward, including *Nude by a Woodland Pool* tentatively dated 1920-22. His original apprenticeship as a lithographer in Breslau spills over in his life's work. His compositions, mainly nudes in landscapes, are characterised by a strong, black outline. Mueller explained that the Egyptian frieze with its emphasis on outline and dark haired, olive-skinned models remained the basis for his conception of the human figure. After World War I and until his death in 1930, Mueller was Professor at the Academy of Fine Arts in Breslau.

Cat. No. 114
Edvard Munch (1863-1944)
The Sick Child (*Das kranke Mädchen*), 1896
Colour lithograph,
41.7 × 56.5 cm (image)
Signed lower right in pencil,
in the border: "E. Munch"
1973.45

"Her eyes became red—I could not believe that death was so inevitable, so near at hand... how strange she felt—the room was different—it was as though she was seeing it through a veil—her body seemed to be weighed down with lead—she was so tired." In his *Family Letters* (c. 1890), (Stang, 1979) Munch described the 1877 death of his favourite sister Sophie, who was then fifteen years old. Munch recalled on several occasions the moving moments of the passing from life to death—the last moments with one's loved ones. Death was a shattering experience to which Munch had been exposed very early in his life. As a consequence, death was a theme which preoccupied him almost to obsession: his mother died in 1868 of tuberculosis shortly after giving birth to his younger sister Inger.

Sophie died in 1877; and his father, with whom he had a strained yet deeply emotional relationship, passed away in 1889. By 1885 Munch was working on his first compositions of death's approach. This is also the year he went to Paris for the first time, and over the period from 1885-86 to c. 1927, he painted six oil and several lithographic versions of *The Sick Child*. This lithograph, of which the Thyssen-Bornemisza print is the earliest, was Munch's most important and was his first colour lithograph. It was done in Paris where Munch stayed in 1896. Traditionally, the sick child represented is thought to be his sister Sophie. The model could very well be the eleven-year-old Betzy Nielsen, whom Munch had seen when accompanying his physician father on a visit in 1885, and who is known to have posed for him. With emotionally-charged paintings such as *The Sick Child* and *The Scream* of 1893 (Nasjonalgalleriet, Oslo), this Nordic loner, perhaps the greatest Norwegian painter of all times, created a form of pictorial language with broad international impact. Each work is touching in intensity and has a particular appeal to young German

artists. Munch spent a lot of time and had several important exhibitions in Germany, particularly Berlin, from the 1890s. *The Scream* was one of the twenty-two paintings included in Munch's large, never finished series "Motifs from the Life of a Modern Soul" (Frieze of Life), with sequences such as "Seeds of Love, Flowering and Passing of Love, Life Anxiety, and Death," parts of which had been exhibited in Berlin in 1892, causing great scandal. The entire series was exhibited in the Berliner Sezession of 1902. Paintings such as *The Scream* express a violent, emotional trauma that nobody who has seen it can ever forget. With these compositions, Munch became one of the greatest influences on the style to develop into German Expressionism. Munch was fiercely independent, stubborn and unsociable. He could never adhere to any artist's group, although he was sollicited and much admired by several artists, associations, including Die Brücke.

Cat. No. 115
Edvard Munch (1863-1944)
Meeting in Space (Begegnung im Weltall), 1899
Three-coloured woodcut on very thin paper, 18.5 × 25 cm (image)
Signed lower right in pencil in the border: "Edv Munch"
1973.44

Love and death occupied Edvard Munch to the point of obsession. His father, a very devout Christian, was deeply saddened by Munch's immoral conduct. He prayed to save his son's soul from the sinful attractions of women, at a time when Norwegian artists of the so-called Christiania-Boheme were advocating and practising free-love. Munch suffered from this conflict with his father. In letters, diaries, and other recollections of his thoughts, Munch described vividly and in detail his perception of life. Munch's six year love affair with the wife of a medical officer in the navy ended only when he went to Paris on a three year visit in 1889, the winter his father died. Shortly after, Munch recalled the vision he had of a loving couple and, although written long before *Meeting in Space*, his description captures the visual impact of this print: "These two in that moment when they are no longer themselves but only one of thousands of links tying one generation to another generation. People should understand the sanctity of this and take off their hats as if they were in church. The chain binding the thousand dead generations to the thousand generations to come is linked together." Another note from 1891 describes, in brief, the ideology of Expressionist paintings: "...In these paintings the painter depicts his deepest emotions, his soul, his sorrows and joys. They display his heart's blood...He depicts the human being, not the object... These paintings are designed to move people intensely, first a few, then more and more, and finally everyone." The couple depicted in *Meeting in Space* is suspended in time and space. Floating around them are spermatozoa which Munch also incorporated in a lithograph version of *Madonna*, c. 1895 (Munch Museum, Oslo). *Madonna* includes with the spermatozoa a skeleton fetus both symbolising life and death. *Meeting in Space* was made from one block sawed into three pieces, and inked bluish green, brick red, and black.

Cat. No. **116**
Sidney Nolan (1917-)
*Study for Constable Fitzpatrick
and Kate Kelly*, 1946
Ripolin on hardboard,
63.5 × 76.3 cm
1980.45

Sidney Nolan is the only Australian artist represented in the Thyssen-Bornemisza Collection. He was
born in Melbourne in 1917 and has
become one of the most celebrated
contemporary Australian artists.
Nolan's formal training was limited to night classes in drawing at
the National Gallery School in
1934. His main purpose for painting, he said, was to transmit emotions and to create emotional communication. In the 1940s, Australian history began to play a role in
Australian art, and Nolan became
its chief exponent. His favourite
subjects were the landscape of
Australia and the continuing saga
of the gangster-hero Ned Kelly.
The Kelly story was based on the

1881 findings of the Royal Commission on the Police Force of Victoria. This story was subsequently
rewritten in *The Complete Inner
History of the Kelly Gang and
their Pursuers* (J. J. Kenneally,
first published in 1929).
The "Kelly" series of twenty-five
paintings, which Nolan began in
1946, became his most famous
work. This epic drama represented, to the outside world, an Australian folk hero in a unique Australian environment. In the film
Nolan at Sixty (1977), the artist
explains the origins of his interest
in the theme of the Kellys: "...it
happens to be true that my grand-
father did chase the Kellys and I
heard all about it from him. He was
a policeman and he was sent up to
Beechwood to chase them. And as
the saying is, it was "double pay
and country girls"—and they
didn't chase the Kellys too hard...
so it was said. They chased the
girls and that's why the Kellys
stayed around for a long time."

Young Kelly was more than an ordinary gangster: He broke the law
as a protest against an unjust society. "Kelly Country" is a portion
of north-eastern Victoria where
Kelly and his gang experienced numerous adventures with the police
until they were finally caught and
killed. The Kelly gang consisted of
Ned Kelly, Kate Kelly and Dan
Kelly, and a number of outlaws.
*Study for Constable Fitzpatrick
and Kate Kelly* is one of two early
studies for the final version of this
scene in the "Kelly Series." The
scene depicts Kate Kelly being ha-
rassed by officer Fitzpatrick while
Ned Kelly, wearing his characteristic black helmet, watches the
scene from a window in the background. Nolan was inspired by Kazimir Malevich's *Black Square*
when inventing the curious black
armour worn by Ned in all the compositions. The series was first
shown in Paris and Rome in 1949
and 1950.

Cat. No. 117
Emil Nolde (Emil Hansen)
(1867-1956)
Summer Flowers (Red and White Poppies against Blue Sky)
([Sommerblumen]
Roter und Weisser Mohn vor blauen Himmel), c. 1930
Watercolour on paper,
45.5 × 33.5 cm
Signed lower right: "Nolde."
1965.5

Born on a farm in Nolde, North Schleswig, in 1867, Emil Hansen's way of painting was slower than that of some of the other German painters of the Expressionist movement. Franz Marc (Cat. No. 107), August Macke (Cat. No. 102) and Egon Schiele (Cat. No. 136), to name but a few, had all achieved major recognition within avant-garde circles while still in their twenties. Nolde was thirty-one when he was rejected admission to the Munich Academy of Art, directed by Franz von Stuck. He was

almost forty before he had his first one-man show at Galerie Ernst Arnold in Dresden (1905). The young artists of the Die Brücke group, and particularly Erich Heckel and Karl Schmidt-Rottluff (Cat. No. 137) admired Nolde's flaming colours and immediately asked him to join the group, which he did in 1906. Since 1903, Nolde and his wife Ada had spent the greater part of the year on the Danish island Alsen where the sky, sea, and flowering gardens provided Nolde with endless subjects. Nolde was the one who introduced the Brücke artists to this part of the Baltic Sea area, and in 1907 invited Schmidt-Rottluff to join him there. By 1906, Nolde had met Edvard Munch (Cat. Nos. 114, 115) in Berlin where he spent the winters. Both artists were loners and had little interest in group activities. Religious subjects became central to Nolde's oeuvre around 1909. His unconventional compositions, nevertheless, were originally refused by the Ber-

lin Sezession. In 1910, therefore, Nolde was one of twenty-seven artists who formed the Neue Sezession. At the Museum of Ethnology in Berlin, Nolde studied primitive sculpture and artifacts, and finally in 1913-14, joined an expedition to New Guinea. Throughout his life, Emil Nolde painted flower compositions—both in oil and watercolour. Spending most summers renting houses or small cottages with flowering gardens, Nolde was able to paint endless variations on the theme. In 1926, Nolde bought a farm in Seebüll, North Frisia, and there he enjoyed some years of peace, relative prosperity, and several public honours before the Nazis made it close to impossible for the German avant-garde painters to paint. The paintings here, including *Summer Flowers (Red and White Poppies against Blue Sky)*, were painted during the calm period at Seebüll, preceding the escalating terror of the Nazi regime.

Cat. No. **118**
Emil Nolde (Emil Hansen)
(1867-1956)
Head of a Woman c. 1925-30
(*Frauenkopf*),
Watercolour on paper,
47 × 34.5 cm
Signed lower right: "Nolde."
1970.34

Cat. No. **119**
Emil Nolde (Emil Hansen)
(1867-1956)
Young Couple (Junges Paar),
c. 1931-35
Watercolour on paper on card,
53.5 × 37 cm
Signed lower right: "Nolde."
1961.3

When Baron Thyssen-Bornemisza bought Emil Nolde's watercolour *Young Couple* in 1961 the Collection—which for about forty years had included solely Old Master paintings—took on a different dimension. Now, thirty years later, the Thyssen-Bornemisza Collection stemming from that one Nolde watercolour, numbers over nine hundred Modern paintings, drawings, and watercolours, almost twice the number of Old Master paintings in the Collection. The Collection counts eleven works by Emil Nolde; those on view are mainly watercolours executed in the decade 1925-35. In *Young Cou-*

ple from 1931-35, cinnabar red, ultramarine, and green in colour, a man and a woman are crudely outlined in black. Nolde here expresses the beauty and the enigma of being a couple where two different personalities/two different characters lead a life together, but also apart. They follow a joint path in life, yet also deviate, and maybe separate along the way. The manner in which Nolde fuses their two heads seems to indicate intellectual understanding. In traditional betrothal paintings the hand symbolises an oath, a promise, an intent. Nevertheless, these young lovers are not staring into one another's eyes, nor looking straight ahead in the same direction, into the same future. Their common future is outside the painting.

Cat. No. **120**
Emil Nolde (Emil Hansen)
(1867-1956)
Iris, Tigerlilies, Poppies
(*Iris, Feuerlilien und Mohn*),
c. 1930-35
Watercolour on paper,
47 × 34 cm
Signed lower right: "Nolde."
1970.31

Cat. No. **121**
Emil Nolde (Emil Hansen),
(1867-1956)
Landscape with Farmhouses
(*Landschaft mit
Bauernhäusern*), 1946-47
Watercolour on paper,
22.5 × 26.3 cm
Signed lower right: "Nolde."
1974.24

sort of St. Peter, Germany on the
North Frisian coast.

With the large retrospective in
Dresden honouring his sixtieth
birthday and his 1931 appointment
to membership in the Prussian
Academy of Fine Arts, Nolde was
established as a major figure in
German painting. Only a few years
later, however, in 1937, 1,052 of his
works were confiscated by the Nazis and exhibited as "degenerate"
art. A year later he started working on his so-called "unpainted"
paintings—mainly flowers. In
1941, he was prohibited from painting altogether. *Landscape with
Farmhouses* was painted shortly
after World War II in the little re-

Cat. No. **122**
Alfonso Angel Ossorio (1916-)
The Cross in the Garden, 1950
Mixed media and collage on
paper, 75.8 × 55.3 cm
Inscribed on verso:
"Cross in the Garden"
1981.3

Alfonso Angel Ossorio was a close
friend of the artist couple Lee
Krasner (Cat. No. 96) and Jackson
Pollock (Cat. Nos. 126-128), and
the painter Jean Dubuffet, all of
whom he had met in 1949. It was
the painting of Pollock and Dubuffet which influenced Ossorio the
most. In 1950 he returned to his island home of Victorias, Negros in
the Phillippines to reconstruct and
redecorate the Chapel of St. Joseph the Worker, originally built
by his family. In several works
relating to this project, Ossorio
represented various studies of
Christ's Passion, of which *The
Cross in the Garden* is one. The influence of Pollock is very obvious;
under a tangle of black and ochre-
yellow lines, one can vaguely dis-
tinguish the figure of Christ on the
Cross against a burning background of red—the colour of passion.

Cat. No. **123**
David Parrish (1939-)
Three Yamahas, 1975
Oil on canvas, 165 × 165 cm
Signed and dated lower right:
"D.Parrish 75"
1976.84

Photo Realism, Hyper or Super Realism was not a "movement" with a set of defined principles and ideas. It was a style widely practised in the United States during the 1970s in which photography and technology were combined to create high-precision paintings of urban landscapes, cars, trucks, motorcycles, and commercial imagery. Included in the 1975 one-man show, "The Motorcycle," at the Sidney Janis Gallery, New York—based on eight models of motorcycles dating from 1972-75—was *Three Yamahas* by David Parrish of Birmingham, Alabama. With almost brutal precision, Parrish, paints the chrome, steel, high polish and shiny metallic colours of three Yamaha motorcycles crammed and cropped in a picture space much too small to contain such a mass of heavy metal. The unnaturally bright light adds to the sparkling cleanliness of image and execution. The close-ups of cut-off detail makes the composition—in isolated parts—appear abstract. Paradoxically, the exactitude of Photo Realism links this style to abstract painting according to Richard Estes (Cat. No. 81), who sees Photo Realism as "an abstract way of seeing things without commentary and personal involvement." The reflections mirrorred on chrome, metal, glass, and windows in the compositions of the Photo Realists became a major part of the technical and visual complexity that makes such works disturbing, provoking, appealing, and/or repulsive.

Cat. No. **124**
Maxfield Parrish (1870-1966)
Villa d'Este, 1903
Oil on board, 71 × 46 cm
Signed with initials lower right:
"M.P."
Inscribed and dated on verso:
"The Oaks Windsor Vermont:
December of 1903. Villa d'Este
Maxfield Parrish."
1979.50

Maxfield Parrish's first cover illustration for *Harper's Bazar* (later *Bazaar*) came out in 1895, and it was as a decorative and commercial artist that Parrish established his fame. His popularity—particularly during the mid-1920s and until around 1930—was such that reproductions of one of his paintings *Daybreak*, 1922 (New York Graphic Society Ltd.), were reported to have hung in a quarter of a million American homes. His style does not place him with any "school" of artists; he concentrated on romantic themes in brilliant colours executed with photographic exactitude. Parrish had a vivid imagination, creating in murals, advertisements and illustrations an idyllic never-never land of Magic Realism. His first commission for book illustrations was *Mother Goose in Prose* by L. Frank Baum, published in 1897, a year before he settled with his wife in Cornish, New Hampshire. In 1903, he was asked by Edith Wharton, whose passion was home decoration and garden landscaping, to illustrate her book *Italian Villas and their Gardens*. That year he toured Italy with the author, making preparatory sketches for the book. The illustrations of the famous grand villas of Campi, Gori, Bello, Medici, Chigi and d'Este, among others, were executed at his home studio, and the book was eventually published in 1910. Villa d'Este, located in the town of Tivoli just outside of Rome, is majestically recessed behind walls of box and laurel, in a garden of cypresses and ilexes.

Parrish developed his own technique, using layers of coloured oil glazes to produce colours of particular depth and brilliance.

Cat. No. **125**
Francis Picabia (Francis Martinez de Picabia)
(1879-1953)
The Grinder (Le Broyeur),
1921-22
Pencil, watercolour and gouache,
60 × 73 cm
Signed lower right:
"Francis Picabia"
Inscribed upper left: "Broyeur"
1976.96

In an interview with a New York reporter of October 1915, Picabia described the impact of his first trip to the United States, saying. "This visit to America...has brought about a complete revolution in my methods of work...Almost immediately upon coming to America it flashed on me that the genius of the modern world is in machinery, and that through machinery art ought to find a most vivid expression." Picabia had already visited New York for the Armory Show in 1913, as the only European "extremist" artist actually present at the epoch-making exhibition. The three paintings by Picabia included in that show, and Picabia's availability to the press and the art circles of New York, made him a sensation. Picabia developed like Marcel Duchamp, a machine inspired, so-called mechanomorphic style motivated by the rapidly growing stage of mechanisation during the second decade of the twentieth century. This was a period in which an abundance of electric equipment came to be owned and operated by the middle classes. These machines included telephones, typewriters, electrical appliances, and cars. Picabia had his first one-man show in Paris in 1905, and was among the foremost avant-garde painters in Paris until World War I. After the War, he collaborated with the Dadaists for a short period between 1918 and 1921. When Tristan Tzara arrived in Paris in 1920 bringing Dada with him, he stayed with Picabia. In 1925, Picabia moved to the South of France, near Mougins and there he lead the mundane life of a celebrated artist. After World War II Picabia went back to Paris and stayed there until his death. *The Grinder* belongs to a group of watercolours on the theme of machinery. It was completed in 1922 and titled on the paper by the artist. "Broyeur" refers to the machine with which a painter grinds his pigments. The circle in black, red, and white—like a wheel or spare part of a machine pulling ropes or wires—occurs frequently in this and other mechanomorphic compositions of the years attributed to his association with the Dadaists.

Cat. No. 126
Jackson Pollock (1912-1956)
Untitled, c. 1945
Pastel, enamel, and sgraffito
on paper, 65 × 52 cm
Signed lower centre:
"Jackson Pollock"
1978.18

Surrealism was one of the most
significant catalysts in the development of Abstract Expressionism which dominated American
painting during the 1940s and
1950s. Abstract Expressionism departed radically from the techniques and concepts of traditional
painting. It discarded the artistic
tradition in which painting is illu-
sionistic. Jackson Pollock studied
with Thomas Hart Benton (Cat.
Nos. 55, 56) — one of the foremost
exponents of Regionalism — from
1930 to 1933. Only few works from
the years with Benton exist, and
they have very little to do with the
style Pollock was later to develop.
The two artists Pollock admired

most were Pablo Picasso and Joan
Miró. The "automatic" compositions of the French Surrealist André Masson (Cat. No. 112) also had
a profound influence on him. Pollock had been in Jungian therapy
and was very interested in the autonomous life of the unconscious — a primary force behind
Surrealism which seeks to approach and represent the deeper
layer of the psyche. Pollock's earliest abstract compositions appeared around 1934-38. In 1943,
Pollock had his first one-man show
at Art of this Century, in which he
was championed as the greatest
painter of our time. Following this
large, important compositions
were bought by the Museum of
Modern Art, New York, and the
San Francisco Museum. At that
point, the artist had already used
his famous technique of pouring
paint directly onto the surface of
his canvases. In the winter of 1946-
47, Pollock took automatism one
step further, and he placed a large

unstretched canvas on the floor on
which he poured, swirled, and
dripped paint. Pollock was hailed
as a shining new phenomenon in
American art, and Abstract Expressionism soon became accepted
as the true avant-garde mode. *Untitled* is one of the first works
where Pollock makes the transi-
tion from the early works retaining
figurative content, to the later drip
paintings that are totally devoid of
visual reference (Cat. No. 128). In
the same year as *Untitled*, Pollock
married Lee Krasner (Cat. No. 96).

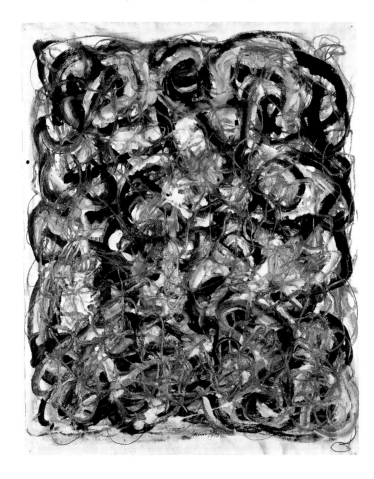

Cat. No. **127**
Jackson Pollock (1912-1956)
Untitled, 1946
Gouache on paper,
56.3 × 77.5 cm
Signed and dated lower right:
"Jackson Pollock 46"
1976.37

Jackson Pollock was often cited his
interest in American Indian art
and sand paintings. He was fascinated by the earth colours and patterns. Any similarity between Pollock's compositions and American
Indian art is, according to the artist, purely accidental. This work is
closely related to the oil painting
Circumcision, 1946 (Peggy Gug-
genheim Collection, Venice). The
triangles, the dominant red tone,
and the dynamically swirling lines
instill a sense of violence and ag-
gression.

Cat. No. **128**
Jackson Pollock (1912-1956)
Number 11, 1950
Oil and aluminium paint on
masonite, 56.5 × 56.5 cm
Signed lower right: "J. Pollock"
Dated lower left "'50"
1975.28

1950 was Jackson Pollock's most
prolific year; he created more than
fifty paintings, and had a very important exhibition at the Betty
Parson's Gallery in New York.
Number 11 was in this exhibition.
The square masonite board on
which Pollock painted *Number 11*
was used only in this particular
year. Pollock gave numbered or informal colour descriptions instead
of verbal titles to his poured paintings in order to avoid creating a visual reference for an abstract
work. He used industrial enamels,
oil and aluminium paints which
shimmer through the web of colours. The period when Pollock
worked exclusively with the method of pouring and dripping paint on
the canvas—called Action Painting—only lasted from 1947 until
1951, upon which the artist rein-
troduced figuration into his work.
From 1945 until his death in a car
accident, Pollock painted very little. He was only forty-four years
old when he died, but his short career can easily be declared one of
the most successful and remarkable in the art of this century.

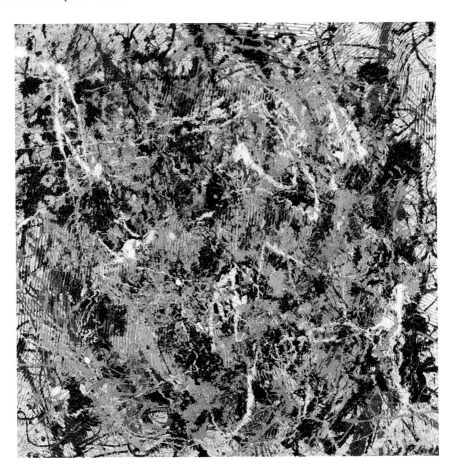

Cat. No. **129**
Stephen Posen (1939-)
Three Cornered Orange, 1973
Oil and acrylic on canvas,
193 × 229 cm
Signed and dated on verso:
"Stephen Posen 1973"
1975.41

The trompe-l'oeil style of Stephen Posen is a variant of Photo or Hyper Realism of the 1970s. The artist does not use photography, but meticulously paints a studio picture of sculptural compositions made out of various-sized boxes. Over these boxes, layers of different coloured materials have been draped or suspended. Posen uses a studio elevator to paint the sections of the painting at eye-height, thereby avoiding distortion. The resulting illusory effect of three—dimensionality is an example of how Photo Realism relates to abstract painting.

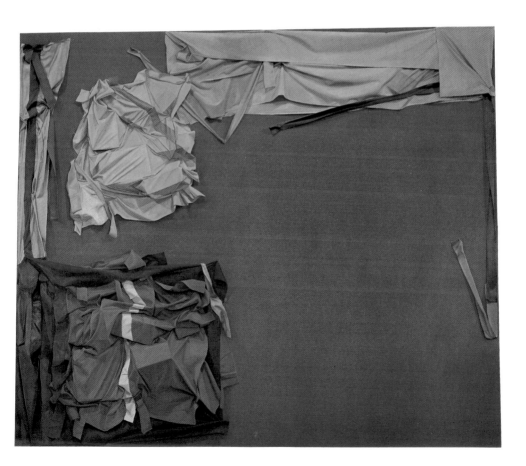

Cat. No. 130
Richard Pousette-Dart
(1916-1992)
Composition, 1946
Oil on canvas, 112 × 94 cm
Signed on a piece of wood
attached to the stretcher:
"R Pousette-Dart"
1975.42

Richard Pousette-Dart appeared
on the New York scene in 1936 and
was one of the Abstract Expressionist artists who made a reputation for himself during the 1940s.
He had important exhibitions at
the Artists Gallery (1941) and the
Betty Parsons Gallery (1948)
where the leading avant-garde
painters of the time, including
Jackson Pollock (Cat. Nos. 126-
128) and Alfonso Ossorio (Cat. No.
122) were shown. Pousette-Dart
was a reflective person who had a
highly developed mystical-philo-
sophical approach to art. He believed that the greater a work of
art was, the more abstract and im-

personal it was. He thought of art
as a beautiful object and a symbol
of experience. *Composition* from
the early years of Abstract Expressionism, resembles a primitive mask, or shield painted in
thickly layered murky colours.
The circle and the eye are used repeatedly within the oval shape of
the "mask," which, in itself symbolises secrecy, mystery, and
magical powers. Pousette-Dart
taught at various art schools and
universities from the end of the
1950s. He was given a major retrospective (1963) and a one-man
show (1974) at the Whitney Museum of American Art, New York,
only to be followed by yet another
successful one-man show at the at
the Indianapolis Museum of Art in
1990.

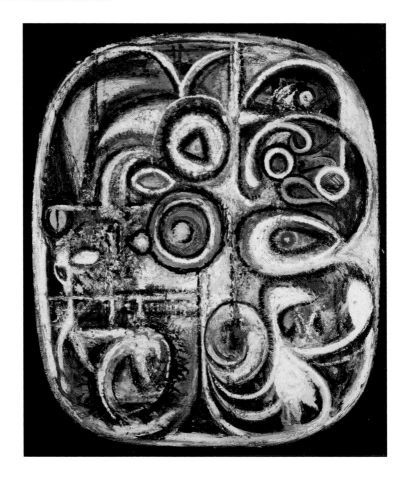

Cat. No. **131**
Bridget Riley (1931-)
Streak 2, 1979
Acrylic on canvas,
116 × 252.5 cm
1980.3

Bridget Riley is an English artist who grew up at the time when American post-war art dominated the English art scene. The major part of her education was during the mid-fifties at the Royal College of Art in London. She started receiving increasing international recognition after participating in the "The Responsive Eye" exhibition at the Museum of Modern Art in New York in 1965, and was awarded the International Prize for Painting at the 34th Venice Biennale. The artist spent her childhood in Cornwall, surrounded by sea, sky, fields, and forest. Her memories of playing on the coast and swimming in the cool, clear waters invade her large-scale paintings with the wavy motif of *Streak 2* which appears in Riley's art between 1967 and throughout the 1970s. In these compositions, Riley recalls the distant impressions of the golden greens of the vegetation growing on the Cornwall cliffs, the red-oranges of seaweed on the blues and violets of adjacent rocks, and the actual magnificent hues of the water according to its depth. In *Streak 2*, these visual memories are translated into optical vibrations of shimmering, flickering colour waves. An interest in Chinese painting during the early and mid-1970s strengthened the abstract meditational qualities of her canvases. Riley's art is clearly defined and limited in her use of impersonal colour, movement, direction, speed, shape, and repetition. Her paintings are not confined to the picture plane but vibrantly fill the distance between the spectator and the canvas.

Cat. No. **132**
William P. Roberts (1895-1980)
Dock Gates, 1920
Oil on canvas, 107 × 137 cm
Signed lower right: "Roberts"
1982.44

William P. Roberts was born in Hackney, London, in 1895. In 1909 he was apprenticed to the advertising firm of Sir Joseph Causton, and attended evening classes at St. Martin's School of Art. From 1910-13, a scholarship allowed Roberts to study art at the Slade School. In 1913 he travelled to Italy and France and painted his first Cubist paintings. During the Spring of 1914, he met Wyndham Lewis, the ingenious painter and writer who originated the English avant-garde movement, Vorticism. Roberts was the youngest of the artists invited to contribute to the first volume of *Blast: Review of the English Vortex*, and to sign the Vorticist manifesto (1914). In the first issue of *Blast*, Vortex was identified as "the point of maximum energy." The ideas expressed could be vaguely described as a combination of Cubist and Futurist principles. Around 1913, these theories led Roberts to participate in the one and only Vorticist Exhibition, in 1915, at the Doré Galleries, London. In the foreword to this exhibition, Lewis defined Vorticism as "Activity, Significance and Essential Movement," and proclaimed that modern art should be "clean, hard and plastic" to fit the mechanical bias of modern culture. Robert's painting *Dock Gates*, executed after World War I, exemplifies Vorticist ideology. He has applied the discipline of geometrical patterning, to a dynamic panorama of industrial activity in London's busy docklands. The composition is literally bursting with activity; a myriad of workers and a multitude of ships cram the picture surface in a celebration to labour and industry. In 1920, Lewis made an unsuccessful attempt at reviving the Vorticist group with the exhibition "Group X" at the Mansard Gallery. Roberts participated in this exhibition. Roberts' association with Vorticism, which can be considered England's first modern movement, is a phase of his career which has been considered particularly significant, and *Dock Gates* is an important example of the essential Vorticist painting. From 1925 Roberts was a teacher at the Central School in London; a position he held until 1960. He lived and worked in London throughout his life except for the war years 1939-45 which he spent in Oxford. Roberts began to exhibit at the Royal Academy in 1948, was elected an Associate in 1958, and subsequently a Royal Academician in 1966. During his long active career Roberts depicted every aspect of ordinary human beings at home, work, at play, and at war—bestowing monumentality to the simplest of scenes.

Cat. No. **133**
Karl Peter Röhl (1890-1975)
Black-Blue (Large Square)
(Schwarz-Blau [Grosses
Quadrat]), 1922
Ink and gouache on paper,
52 × 38.5 cm
Signed and dated lower left:
"Karl Peter Röhl 1922."
1986.19

Karl Peter Röhl was one of the first artists who studied at the Weimar art school into which the Berlin architect Walter Gropius, in 1919, transformed the experimental Bauhaus School. At the Bauhaus, the functions of an art academy and a school of applied arts were combined for the first time. The five-year program aimed at introducing students to theory and practice; the aesthetic and the utilitarian; and the many different aspects of creative expression such as fine arts, furniture design, architecture, ceramics, weaving, theatre, and costume design. The ambition was to bridge the gap between fine and applied arts as well as to elevate the standards of industrial design. Gropius engaged a handful of outstanding avant-garde artists to teach at the Bauhaus, including Johannes Itten (Cat. No. 93), Lyonel Feininger, Paul Klee, Wassily Kandinsky and Oskar Schlemmer. Soon the Bauhaus attracted enthusiastic and talented pupils, one of them being Karl Peter Röhl. Röhl met Theo van Doesburg, the founder of the Dutch Constructivist group De Stijl, when van Doesburg came to visit Weimar in 1920. From 1921 until 1923, van Doesburg directed a design course at the Bauhaus based on the non-figurative form and colour principles of De Stijl. Röhl and Walter Dexel (Cat. No. 72) were among the staunch supporters of Doesburg and his ideas. Röhl eventually published constructivist drawings in Doesburg's art magazine *De Stijl. Black-Blue (Large Square)* was illustrated in *De Stijl*—and belongs to the important series of works executed between the Bauhaus years of 1921 and 1925. Straight horizontal and vertical black lines; the bright unmodulated primary colours; red, yellow, blue, and white are the characteristic principles of works belonging to De Stijl. The art of Röhl reveals also the influence of Feininger, his first teacher at the Bauhaus, and the Russian Suprematist Constructivists Malevich and El Lissitzky. Among the projects Röhl realised in Weimar during the Bauhaus years were the decoration of the Weimar Theatre, a bar, a home for children and a home for the elderly. When Röhl left the Bauhaus in 1926 he was appointed to the Städel Institut in Frankfurt am Main, where he stayed until he was expelled by the Nazis in 1942. He returned to his native Kiel after World War II, and lived there until his death in 1975.

Cat. No. **134**
Olga Vladimirovna Rozanova
(1886-1918)
Urban Landscape, 1912
Oil on cardboard, 61 × 51 cm
1980.25

Olga Vladimirovna Rozanova, wasborn in Melenki, Vladimir Province and attended the Bolshakov Art School (1904-12), and the Stroganov Industrial Art Institute (arts and crafts) both in Moscow. She moved to St. Petersburg in 1911 where she came in contact with the Union of Youth group. In her very short life—she died prematurely of diphtheria in 1918— Rozanova participated in almost every major exhibition of the Russian Avant-Garde and was among the first to become associated with the Russian Futurist movement. Rozanova was a painter as well as a poet. She intimately related to the leading poets of the period. Her marriage in 1916 to the poet Alexei Kruchenykh, one of the creators of

modern Russian Futurist poetry, furthered her interest in the design of books, especially volumes of poetry. Through working with her husband on his books *The War* and *The Universal War* (1916), she arrived at some of the earliest examples of non-objective compositions in Russia, independently of Wassily Kandinsky and Kazimir Malevich (Cat. No. 103). Rozanova had already met Malevich in 1913 in conjunction with the Union of Youth group in St. Petersburg. They were both members. She associated herself with Suprematism from the time of the "Last Futurist Exhibition 0.10" in St. Petersburg (1915) where Malevich showed his Suprematist works for the first time. Together, with other supporters such as Ivan Kliun, Ivan Puni, and Nadezhda Udaltsova (Cat. Nos. 146, 147), Rozanova and Malevich formed the Supremus group. After the Revolution, Rozanova worked with Alexander Rodchenko in organising art

schools and art workshops to produce textiles, ceramics, woodwork, and printed materials. Her paintings of 1912-14, to which *Urban Landscape* belongs, are a combination of Cubism and Futurism with a specific Russian variant of those styles called Cubo-Futurism. In *Urban Landscape* and other city views of the period, the diagonal is the predominant organising element. *Urban Landscape* is painted in a Cubist tonality of brown, grey, white, and black. The paint is applied as dynamic rays shooting across the picture surface in a manner somewhat similar to Italian Futurist compositions. It has been suggested by John Bowlt that *Urban Landscape* is a study for Rozanova's *Cityscape* (c. 1913).

Cat. No. **135**
John Singer Sargent (1856-1925)
Perseus by Night, c. 1907
Watercolour on paper,
54.6 × 39.3 cm
1978.22

John Singer Sargent's bravura portraits of dazzling socialites mirrored social history in Europe and the United States for almost forty years, and established Sargent as the most brilliant portrait painter of his time. Sargent—who was an American citizen, but spent almost all his life in Paris and London—studied portraiture under E. C. Carolus-Duran at the Ecole des Beaux Arts in Paris in 1874, and quickly excelled in the genre to become the master's star pupil. Two years later—when Impressionism was coming to the fore—Sargent met Claude Monet. The two artists were to become very close friends around a decade later. Sargent was among the first expatriate American artists to adopt the Im-pressionist technique, and he was instrumental in introducing the aesthetic to an American audience. While portrait painting continued to be Sargent's primary occupation, he produced outstanding landscapes and became a virtuoso watercolour painter, particularly after 1900. In 1903-04, Venetian architectural and sculptural motifs had been the subject of some superb watercolour sketches, and this subject would continue to fascinate him over the years. *Perseus by Night*, c. 1907, was part of a series of studies of Cellini's bronze sculpture *Perseus* in the Loggia dei Lanzi in Florence, where Sargent was born. Sargent's watercolours were much appreciated in the United States, and helped foster a general American interest in watercolour as an artistic medium.

Cat. No. **136**
Egon Schiele (1890-1918)
Boy in a Sailor Suit
(*Paul Erdmann*), (*Knabe im*
Matrosenanzug), 1915
Graphite, wax crayon and oil
paint on paper, 47.5 × 31.5 cm
Signed and dated lower right, in
cartouche: "Egon Schiele 1915"
1974.18

Paul Erdmann was the nephew of
Edith Harms and a model for several of Egon Schiele's drawings
and gouaches during the autumn of
1915, the year that Schiele and
Harm wed. Their union lasted a
short three years; Edith contract-
ed the Spanish flu and died in October, 1918. Schiele died a few weeks
later, inflicted with the same epi-
demic. By then, he had achieved
major national and international
success. Schiele was born in Tullin
on the Danube not far from Vienna. His talents were recognised
early and he was sent to study at
the Vienna Academy of Fine Arts

in 1907, where he only stayed until
1909. Schiele's controversial art,
highly criticised for its erotic content, caused a public uproar. The
artist spent a few days in prison
charged with sexual misconduct
and corruption of minors, as he often used very young girls for models. He was, however, released for
lack of proof. Although public out-
rage sometimes forced him to relo-
cate, he found many supporters
among fellow artists—principally
Gustav Klimt—and important col-
lectors. The number of exhibitions
Schiele participated in at home and
abroad is astonishing for his young
age, as well as clear proof of his
broad recognition. The atmosphere of Vienna at the time he
emerged was ripe for the acknowl-
edgement and exploration of the
deeper impulses of human nature.
This time paralleled Sigmund
Freud's publications on the human
psyche and his practice of psycho-
analysis. The ambiance was fruit-
ful in fostering the art of Klimt,

and in turn Schiele, with its morbid and passionate introspection,
which Austrians were perhaps un-
easy, but quite proud to have been
the first to bring to the surface.
Schiele's gifts as a draughtsman
and portraitist were undeniable
even to his enemies. In this portrait of the budding teenager Paul
Erdmann, the economy and assur-
ance of line is remarkable: not one
stroke has been reworked, reen-
forced or rethought. The three-
quarter profile has the freshness
and softness of the young man's
face, whereas the sailor suit and
the bare, bony knees are those of a
child.

Cat. No. **137**
Karl Schmidt-Rottluff
(1884-1976)
The Village of Dangast
(*Dorf Dangast*), 1909
Watercolour on paper,
52.5 × 65.5 cm
Signed and dated lower right:
"S. Rottluff 1909"
1970.28

Karl Schmidt-Rottluff was born in Rottluff, Germany, the name of his native town. He was the youngest of the four painters who in 1905 founded the Die Brücke group (The Bridge) in Dresden and with it, set German Expressionism on its course. The name Brücke was suggested by Schmidt-Rottluff. The other painters were Erich Heckel. Fritz Bleyl and Ernst Ludwig Kirchner. The group exhibited for the first time in Leipzig in 1905 and then in 1906 at the Dresden lamp factory of the collector Seifert. The early work of Schmidt-Rottluff was heavily influenced by Vincent van Gogh and the Impressionists. Colours and thick, gestural brushwork had the explosive intensity and clashing colour constellations of Expressionism. In 1906, Schmidt-Rottluff

discovered Dangast in the province of Oldenburg on the North Sea and the spent every summer painting there until 1912. The many landscapes in oil and watercolour which he produced during the summers in Dangast belong to the most important works of his early oeuvre. While Schmidt-Rottluff's oil paintings executed in and around Dangast are characterised by a thick, crusty paint layer, the artist's watercolours of 1909, when *The Village of Dangast* was painted, are looser, and lighter, and more luminous. The peaceful fields and houses of the village vibrate with undulating waves of colour, releasing the sensation of cosmic energy. This watercolour was included in the exhibition of works by artists of Die Brücke at the Kunstsalon Richter in Dresden in 1909. Their works, refused by the Berliner Sezession, forced the Brücke artists to form the Neue Sezession in Berlin in 1911, where Schmidt-Rottluff settled and continued to live for the greater part of his life. From 1913, the year the Die Brücke group was dissolved, his paintings took on a monumental simplicity, concentrating on crude outline, and a language con-

sisting of symbolic shapes. The influence of African sculpture is manifested in Schmidt-Rottluff's work from this period onward. After World War I, the artist continued to work and gave more importance to watercolours from the year 1923. In 1931 he became, a member of the Prussian Academy of Fine Arts. Paintings by Schmidt-Rottluff were included in the "Degenerate Art" exhibition in Munich in 1937, and all works by the artist in German museums were confiscated in 1938, followed by a prohibition to paint in 1941. When his Berlin studio was destroyed by bombing in 1943 he moved to Rottluff and lived there until after the War. From 1947 he was Professor at the Art Academy in Berlin. He continued to paint well into his late eighties. Throughout his life the artist had many group and one man exhibitions all over Germany, but very few elsewhere.

Cat. No. **138**
Arthur Segal (1875-1944)
Bridge (Volen-Damm), 1921
Oil on canvas and wood frame,
85.5 × 105.5 cm
1978.80

Arthur Segal worked his way towards Abstraction through Fauvism, Neo-Impressionism, and Expressionism. Within the artistic milieu of Pre- and Post-World War I Berlin, he held a position as a respected, progressive artist and talented teacher who never formally belonged to any prevailing trend or group. In 1920, Segal became affiliated with the November Group with which the majority of progressive Post-War Berlin artists exhibited. His painting schools and his homes — Berlin during the twenties and later, London in 1936 — became gathering places for artists, art students, writers, dancers, and psychologists. In London Segal pioneered — with the support of Sigmund Freud — an art-therapy program within the Arthur Segal Painting School for Professionals and Non-Profession-

als. *Bridge* was painted in 1921, after a summer sojourn in Ruegenwaldermuende on the Baltic Sea. The painting was exhibited in his first retrospective exhibition (1896-1921) at the Josef Altmann Kunsthandlung und Antiquariat, Berlin, in December 1921. The exhibition included a total of twenty-four, mainly Expressionist paintings from 1896 to 1917 and twenty-six Equivalence paintings from 1917-1921, of which *Bridge* was number forty-four. The Equivalence paintings were met with cautious praise for their unconventional exploration of colour theories, mainly those of Goethe and Delaunay, but critised for attempting to express a dogmatic scientific program at the expense of pure painting. Segal made the first attempts at dividing the picture plane into square or rectlinear compartments which, in 1917, eventually spilled over onto the picture frame itself. These compositions were called Equivalence paintings by the artist, thus referring to his efforts to distribute equal visual importance to each

part of the composition — even the frame. The idea of continuing the composition onto the frame had been introduced by Georges Seurat (1886). In these paintings, Segal fragmented the motif into geometric compartments with a prismatic distortion of the subject matter similar to the effect of a kaleidoscope. Segal used a limited range of tonal graduations of blues, browns and beiges which he systematically applied to the canvas. His art is very personal and had no direct followers. Even his most famous pupil, Cesar Domela (Cat. No. 73), has a radically different style from that of his teacher. Segal left this type of painting and, for the last fifteen years of his life, he returned to figurative works.

Cat. No. **139**
Gino Severini (1883-1966)
Still-Life with Marsala
(Natura Morta al Marsala), 1917
Oil on panel, 46 × 33 cm
Signed lower left: "G. Severini"
1976.10

While studying at the Villa Medici in Rome in 1901, Gino Severini, originally from Cortona, met Umberto Boccioni and Giacomo Balla, the leaders-to-be of the Italian Futurist movement. When Severini settled in Paris in 1906, he befriended Pablo Picasso. He became actively involved with the Futurist movement and was among the five artists who signed the Futurist Manifesto in 1910. The 1910s were particularly creative years for Severini when a period of compositions along the principles of Futurism were followed by a period of assimilation of Cubist theories. Severini managed to create a compromise between the light, movement, and colour-dynamics of Fu-

turism, and the multiple perspective of Cubism. A series of classic Cubist still-life works of the years referred to above includes the painting *Still-Life with Marsala*. The composition combines a bottle of Marsala wine, a glass, a guitar, and a copy of de Stendhal's *de l'A-mour* placed on a table. Severini's application of Cubist principles is refined and balanced, comparable to that of Picasso, Georges Braque, and Juan Gris. Severini breaks up the shapes of the various objects into simple, geometric patterns. His use of dots and stylised wood or marble is typical of the artist's work of this period. These Cubist still-lifes lifes count as the finest of Severini's early oeuvre. The 1920s, quite abruptly, brought about a return to more classical figurative, naturalistic subjects. In a comparable still-life of 1920 *Still-Life with Bottle of Wine* (Otterlo, Rijksmuseum Kröller-Müller, The Netherlands) all traces of Cubism have disappeared.

Cat. No. **140**
Gino Severini (1883-1966)
*Rhythm of the pas de deux
at the Opéra (Ritmo di pas de
deux all'Opéra)*, 1950
Oil on canvas, 116 × 89 cm
Signed lower right: "G. Severini"
1976.27

After World War II and during the
1950s, Gino Severini worked on
several theatre and stage designs
and painted a number of compositions on the theme of the Comme-
dia dell'Arte figures: Pierrot, Har-
lequin, et. al. *Rhythm of the pas de
deux at the Opéra* falls into this period of Severini's production and is
executed in the planar, Cubo-Ab-
stract manner of Severini's later
years. The greater part of the composition is a play of black and red
outlines, isolated on the white
ground of the canvas and desig-
nating areas coloured with tones of
salmon, green, and grey. The composition shows a series of swirling
movements and vaguely recognisable parts of the ballerina's tutu or
the limbs of the male ballet dancer.
Severini made several large fres-
coes and murals for churches and
public buildings in his native country of Italy and elsewhere during
the later years of his life. He died
in Paris in 1966.

Cat. No. **141**
Ben Shahn (1898-1969)
Riot on Carol Street, 1944
Tempera on board, 71 × 51 cm
Signed lower right: "Ben Shahn"
1977.10

The 1930s were years of financial distress in America. After the great stock market crash of 1929, the Depression ravaged the existence of millions of workers in all sectors of American economical life. Unemployment and misery soared. Relief programs were set up in many professions to stem poverty. Many artists working during the 1930s found federal employment as decorators of great public buildings and spaces. Ben Shahn, who had a strong background in graphic communications, enrolled in the 1934 Public Works of Art Project. Shahn's sympathies were always with the working class and the urban poor. His style reflects a concern for social and human justice. Shahn's paintings are marked by a graphic simplicity that carries an easily read message: *Riot on Carol Street* contrasts a tiny group of angry, gesticulating female workers outside a huge, imposing factory building. From their protected, elevated position inside the building the managers are passive spectators—as in a theatre—to the drama of human indignation. The trademark of Shahn's art continued to be this type of intense and political engagement. Just before he died in 1969, Shahn witnessed the student revolts and opernly condemned the war in Vietnam.

Cat. No. 142
Charles Sheeler (1883-1965)
Ore Into Iron, 1953
Tempera on plexiglass,
23 × 17.5 cm
1973.8

Charles Sheeler was one of William Merritt Chase's most promising students at the Pennsylvania Academy of Fine Arts. From 1908 to 1910 he moved on to study art in Europe, mainly Paris, and returned with a first-hand knowledge of the latest trends in painting Cubism, Fauvism, and the work of Cézanne. In Philadelphia, and later New York, Sheeler became affiliated with a group of painters called the Precisionists. During the 1920s this group specialised in glorified images of industrial structures and an idealised vision of progress and prosperity through machines and factories. Other leading members of this group included Georgia O'Keeffe, Charles Demuth (Cat. Nos. 69-71)

and Stuart Davis (Cat. No. 68). Behind the theory of Precisionism were Cubist ideas, assimilated through contact with French artists. The formal approach of the Precisionist painters included a search for precise interpretations, mainly of industrial architecture with its skyscrapers, factories, steel mills, bridges, and oil refineries. The subject was painted flawlessly and meticulously detached in order to create a sensation of machine-like perfection. Sheeler had worked for a living as a photographer since 1912 and became a master photographer of urban and industrial scenes to the extent that his commercial photography work allowed him little time to paint. He started to use photographs as models for idealised visions of American functionalism during the early 1920s. *Ore Into Iron*, 1953, like many of his compositions, is based on photographs and represents the blast furnaces of Pittsburgh. There are several

closely related compositions in the 1957 series "Continuity," of which some, like *Ore into Iron*, are executed in the peculiar technique of tempera on plexiglass.

Cat. No. **143**
Charles Sheeler (1883-1965)
*Composition Around Yellow
No. 2*, 1958
Tempera on paper, 12 × 16.3 cm
Signed and dated lower right:
"Sheeler. 1958"
1973.7

When Charles Sheeler, rented a
barnhouse in Bucks County, outside Philadelphia, in 1910, he had
the opportunity to familiarise himself with Shaker arts and crafts.
He became instantly attracted to
the highly structured harmony between form and function of Shaker
architecture, furniture, and utensils. A disciplined, almost compul-
sory search for defining the essen-
tiality of forms within the basic geometric structure of objects—
which is very similar to the Shaker
spirit—marked Sheeler's own approach to painting. The industrial,
rural, and urban landscapes which
formed the quasi-totality of his
paintings—until a stroke in 1959

left him incapable of painting anymore—became increasingly pure
and reduced to a near abstract
quality. In *Composition Around
Yellow, No. 2*, one of Sheeler's last
paintings, the play of overlapping
planes produce transparent and
opaque colour zones that serve to
bring out the lucidity of the yellow
Shaker barn facade and the yellow
sky above. While Sheeler's art
emanates from the admiration for
American engineering and technology and a puritan submission to
order, it also reveals "the influence
of the [American] Protestant mind
on Cubism" (Hilton Kramer, in
Artforum, Vol. 7, January 1969,
pp. 36-39). Sheeler's works illustrate what happens when Cubist
technique is separated from Cubist
philosophy.

Sheeler-1958

Cat. No. 144
Saül Steinberg (1914-)
Ingresso Air Mail, 1970
Watercolour, crayon and collage
on paper, 49.5 × 64.5 cm
Signed and dated lower right:
"Steinberg 1970"
1980.63

Saül Steinberg is, above all, an artist of the free imagination. He
states: "I am among the few who
continue to draw after childhood is
ended, continuing and perfecting
childhood drawing—without the
traditional interruption of academic training." The large majority of
his paintings, collages, and cartoons executed since he started
working for the *New Yorker* magazine in 1941, present the absurd,
funny, and grotesque aspects of
the average New Yorker's daily
life and environment. Steinberg
left his native Roumania, which he
called a "Masquerade Country," in
1933, to spend six years in Milan,
studying architecture. There, he
made a living by publishing cartoons. About his training and work
in Milan, Steinberg said: "The
study of architecture is a marvel-
ous training for anything but architecture. The frightening thought
that what you draw may become
a building makes for reasoned
lines...In Fascist Italy, where the
controlled press was extremely
boring, the humour magazines
were a way of knowing other aspects of life, which by the nature of
humour itself, seemed subver-
sive." (Quoted from the catalogue
of Saül Steinberg's retrospective
at the Whitney Museum of American Art, New York, 1978.) The
war forced him to leave Europe
and, in 1942, he arrived in New
York. Being an immigrant, like Richard Lindner (Cat. No. 101), with
whom he formed a close friendship, affected his work and outlook
on himself and his new country-
men. Steinberg's compositions
communicate with the signs and
symbols of our age and heritage.

His assemblage series "Air Mail"
was produced over the years 1969-
72. In *Ingresso Air Mail*, Steinberg aesthetically arranges an en-
trance stub and an Italian newspaper cutting into a fanciful play of
the red, white and blue stripes of
an airmail envelope, which recalls
the collage compositions Pablo Picasso and Kurt Schwitters. Steinberg's work has always been very
popular, and he has had many one-
man exhibitions all over the United States, Europe, and South
America.

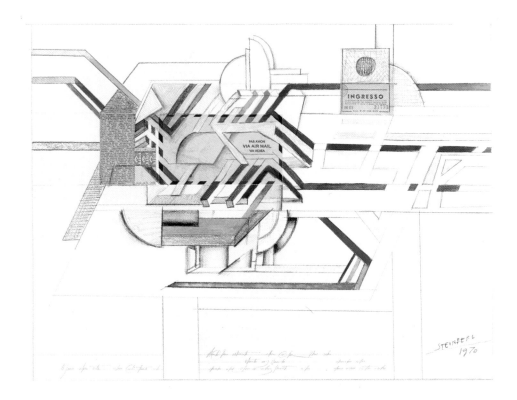

Cat. No. 145
Varvara Fedorovna Stepanova
(1894-1958)
Two Figures at a Table, 1921
Tempera and pencil on paper,
28.7 × 28.5 cm
Signed in Russian and dated
lower right: "Varst 21"
1983.28

Varvara Fedorovna Stepanova moved to Moscow in 1912 from Kazan where she had studied at the Kazan Art School with the Avant-Garde artist Alexander Rodchenko, whom she married in 1913. The couple attended the Stroganov Central Industrial Art Institute in Moscow (1913-14) and participated in important Avant-Garde exhibitions, including the Society of Young Artists which first exhibited in 1919, the X State Exhibition "Non-Objective Creativity and Suprematism," also in 1919, and the 1921 Constructivist "5 × 5 = 25" exhibition in Moscow under the auspices of the Institute of Artistic

Culture (Ginkhuk). Besides Stepanova and Rodchenko, who were at the forefront of the Russian Avant Garde movement through the 1920s, the three other artists each represented in the exhibition with five works were, Alexandra Exter (Cat. No. 82), Liubov Popova and Alexander Vesnin. Stepanova participated in the "First Russian Art Exhibition" in Berlin in 1922. That same year, she made costume designs for theatre performances. From 1923 she was working with Rodchenko and Popova on textile designs for the Moscow First State Textile Factory and became Professor of the Textile Department at the Vkhutemas (Higher Art Technical Studios) from 1924-25. In 1925 she participated in the Paris "Exposition Internationale des Arts Décoratifs et Industriels." From the mid-1920s, Stepanova worked mainly on typography, set designs and posters. *Two Figures at a Table* dates from the beginning of the period where Stepano-

va was increasingly concerned with human figure studies adapted into theatre costume and textile designs. The composition shows two robot-like seated figures, talking and gesticulating around a table. The figures are reduced to flat, angular shapes and coloured patterns. During the 1930s, Stepanova also worked on the propaganda magazine *USSR in Construction*.

Cat. No. 146
Nadezhda Udaltsova (1886-1961)
Composition, 1916
Pencil, watercolour and gouache
on brown wrapping paper,
46.8 × 37.8 cm
1980.26

Nadezhda Udaltsova was one of the important female artists in the Russian Avant-Garde movement. She had settled with her family in Moscow in 1892 and studied painting both at the Moscow Institute of Painting, Sculpture, and Architecture; and at Konstantin Yuon's private art school (1906). While at Yuon's studio, Udaltsova first saw the Impressionist and Post-Impressionist collections of Morozov and Shchukin. These included spectacular paintings by all the major Impressionists and works by Paul Gauguin, Paul Cézanne, Vincent van Gogh and Pablo Picasso. She attended the studio of Kiss in 1909, and left in 1911 with her painter friend Liubov Popova for Paris with ambitions to study Cubism at La Palette, the studio of Jean Metzinger, Emile-Eugène Fauconnier, and Andre Denoyer de Segonzac. Upon her return to Russia, Udaltsova was a full-fledged Cubist. The Cubist phase of her work lasted until 1919 and is particularly important in her creative development. Although Udaltsova worked mainly as a Cubist, she was also interested in Suprematism (1915-16), particularly during the period in which she was closely associated with Ivan Klyun, Kazimir Malevich (Cat. No. 103), Popova, Olga Rozanova (Cat. No. 134), and Vladimir Tatlin. Udaltsova worked at Tatlin's studio The Tower in 1913, and took part in radical leftist exhibitions such as "Jack of Diamonds" in Moscow in 1914; "Tramway V" in St. Petersburg in 1915; and "The Store" in Moscow in 1916. Like many Avant-Garde artists Udaltsova welcomed the Revolution and went to work for the Soviets and for the People's Commissariat for Enlightenment, on the reorganisation of the art educational programs and facilities. During the 1920s and 1930s, Udaltsova returned to figural compositions, portraits, still-lifes and landscapes inspired by Cézanne and the Impressionists. The influence of Malevich and his theory of Suprematism is very clear in Udaltsova's abstract compositions of the years 1916-17. *Composition*, painted in 1916, depicts flat, geometrical forms and angular, overlapping planes in primary colours—like pieces of different coloured papers placed on top of one another.

Cat. No. **147**
Nadezhda Udaltsova (1886-1961)
Untitled, 1917
Gouache, watercolour and pencil
on heavy paper, 36 × 25 cm
Signed and dated lower left in
Russian: "N Udaltsova 1917"
1977.105

Untitled is another example of the
style characteristic of Nadeshda
Udaltsova's work of the years from
1913-19, in which she was exces-
sively prolific. The composition reveals her assimilation of Kazimir
Malevich's theories of Suprematism: relying on flat, simple, non-
figurative shapes. Through colour relationships the overlapping
planes seem to float, gyrate, or collide in open and uncrowded space.
The elegantly balanced forms and
bold colours lend Udaltsova's little
composition a delightfully decorative aspect.

Cat. No. 148
Maria Ivanovna Vasilieva
(Marie Vassilieff), (1884-1957)
Woman with a Fan
(*Femme à l'éventail*), 1910
Oil on canvas, 60 × 72.5 cm
1978.79

Marie Vassilieff was born in Smolensk in 1884. She began studying medicine in St. Petersburg in 1902, but soon switched to painting at the Academy of Art. The artist received a grant to travel to Paris in 1905. In 1907, she settled in Paris, and studied for a while with Henri Matisse. In Paris Vassilieff also worked as a Russian correspondent. In 1908, she founded the short-lived Académie Russe and, in 1909, the Académie Vassilieff — which became the meeting place for painters such as Georges Braque, Juan Gris, Henri Matisse, Amedeo Modigliani, Pablo Picasso, and visiting Russian artists. Ferdinand Léger was among the famous artists giving conferences at her aca-

demy. Vassilieff participated in most of the Paris "Salons" from 1909 onward. In 1914, she travelled to Scandinavia, Poland, Rumania, and Russia. Upon her return to France, she volunteered for Red Cross ambulance service. Vassilieff opened a canteen in Paris for artists in distress and, in 1917, was placed under surveillance as a Russian emigrée. Vassilieff exhibited in New York in 1915, and in London in 1920. During the years 1924 to 1937, she made numerous stage and costume designs. Between 1928 and 1930, the artist had major exhibitions in London and Italy. During World War II, she lived in the South of France. Upon her return to Paris in 1945, she could no longer firmly reestablish her former privileged position in Paris art circles. She retired to the House of the Artists in Nogent-sur-Marne where she died in 1952. A retrospective of Vassilieff's work was held in Paris in 1957. Another important exhibition of her Cubist

works from 1908 to 1915 was held at the Galerie Hupel, Paris in 1969. This exhibition included *Woman with a Fan* of 1910 — the year after the artist had founded the Académie Vassilieff. There is very little trace of the training Vassilieff originally received from Matisse, except perhaps for the joyous dash of colour in the fruit arrangement in the centre of the painting. *Woman with a Fan* is a classical Cubist painting of a lady with a fan and a lute. There is no separation between the motif and the space around the objects. The whole surface of the composition is crammed with angular fragments of the motif, depicted at different distances and at different angles.

Cat. No. **149**
Max Weber (1881-1961)
New York, 1913
Oil on canvas, 101.6 × 81.3
Signed and dated lower left:
"MAX WEBER '13"
1977.112

From 1905 to 1917 an avant-garde movement developed in New York, to a large extent prompted by the exhibition activities of the photographer Alfred Stieglitz, who was known to promote European and American artists at his Gallery at 291 Fifth Avenue. Cézanne, Pablo Picasso, and Henri Matisse could be seen there, as well as young American artists such as John Marin (Cat. Nos. 108, 109) and Max Weber. Weber studied under Matisse during his 1905 stay in Paris and had also met Picasso, Henri Rousseau and Robert Delaunay. He returned to New York in 1909 with a personal version of Cubism and Fauvism apparent in *New York*, of 1913—the year of the historic Armory Show in New York. Weber is remarkable as a precursor of American abstraction. He concentrated on depictions of New York; the big city with its skyscrapers and pulsating energy, and adopted, from Cubism, a fragmented and multiple viewpoint of the scene/object. Although fragments of skyscrapers with rows of windows are recognisable in *New York*, the composition does point towards a total disintegration of the identifiable object, and as such towards abstraction.

Cat. No. **150**
Tom Wesselmann (1931-)
Drawing for Banner Nude,
c. 1968
Pencil and liquitex on Bristol
board, 21.5 × 39 cm
Signed along lower left side:
"Wesselmann ca 68"
1976.54

Tom Wesselmann is most famous for his "Great American Nudes," begun in 1961. While studying psychology at the local University of Cincinnati, Ohio, in the early 1950s, he began selling cartoons and decided to study art in New York at Cooper Union where he graduated in 1959. Like Roy Lichtenstein, James Rosenquist, and Andy Warhol, who also used commercial billboard imagery during the 1960s, Wesselmann was called a Pop artist, although he resented this labelling. The object of Wesselmann's "Great American Nude" and "Bedroom" series is a gorgeous, young, reclining nude—or parts of her—viewed at an erotically close range. Wesselmann draws with hard edges and clean, clear lines and paints with flat, bright colours. In both *Drawing for Banner Nude*, c. 1968 and *Open End Nude Drawing*, 1974, Wesselmann cuts off the limbs and hair of the suntanned girl, sprawled across the horizontal composition. She is "dressed" in the bikini stripes of her suntan or black stockings in the case of *Drawing for Banner Nude*. The artist executed a large number of variations on the theme of the "Great American Nude" where the woman is represented as the depersonalised object of sexual desire.

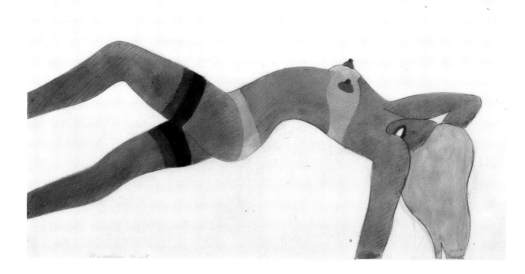

Cat. No. **151**
Tom Wesselmann (1931-)
Open End Nude Drawing, 1974
Stencil with pencil and
watercolour, 10 × 22.5 cm
Signed and dated lower left:
"# 70 Wesselmann 74"
1976.85

Cat. No. **152**
Tom Wesselmann (1931-)
Bedroom Collage, 1974
Pencil, liquitex and collage
on board, 11.5 × 21.5 cm
Signed and numbered upper left:
"Wesselmann 12/20"
1977.37

As one of an edition of twenty,
the small-scale *Bedroom Collage* is
similar to the larger oil painting of
1968, *Bedroom Painting No. 6.*
The collage features a close-up of
a woman's breast in an interior.
Through the window one sees a
view of the New York skyline. The
photos of orange and yellow daffo-
dils are obvious symbols of fertil-
ity, whereas a piece of leopard skin
alludes both to the feline characteristics of women, and luxury.
The viewer is so close to the model's breast that he cannot see the
woman. Her disappearance contrasts the distant world outside
which is depicted with postcard
clarity.

Cat. No. **153**
Andrew Wyeth (1917-)
Malamute, 1976
Watercolour on paper,
79 × 137 cm
Signed lower right:
"Andrew Wyeth"
1977.84

Andrew Wyeth, son of the painter Newell Convers Wyeth (Cat. No. 154), still lives in his childhood home of Chadds Ford, Pennsylvania. His upbringing, strongly influenced by his father, was a nurturing and creatively expressive one. Wyeth's artistic achievements surpassed that of his father's, and he ranks today as one of America's most popular living artists. Although the art of Andrew Wyeth follows the Realist tradition of Winslow Homer (Cat. Nos. 25, 26) and Edward Hopper (Cat. Nos. 90-92), with whom he is often likened, the term Magic Realism is more appropriate, referring to the unique context and magic am-biance in which figures and objects are depicted with almost photographic likeness. The strength and particular refinement of Wyeth's figural or landscape compositions lie in the fact that he creates an un-nerving tension—a lingering antic-ipation of something intangible, not-yet-defined—Wyeth executes the image in the most meticulous of manners. In *Malamute*, the ambiguous relationship between the two wolf-like dogs is one that suggests both a friendly pair and threatening enemies. The wild dogs are silhouetted against an expanse of snow, and contrast with the neat fences of civilised life. Wyeth prefers working with tempera or watercolour, and kept to a subdued tonal scale of grey or earthen colours.

Cat. No. **154**
Newell Convers Wyeth
(1882-1945)
Farm, c. 1916
Oil on canvas, 152.4 × 182.9 cm
Signed lower left:
"N.C. WYETH"
1978.59

Like Maxfield Parrish (Cat. No. 124), Newell Convers Wyeth studied for a while with the great illustrator Howard Pyle and became particularly successful as a commercial and decorative artist. He painted over two thousand illustrations for books, magazines, posters, and advertisements. He also received several commissions to paint murals for public buildings. While commercial work secured good earnings, Wyeth's real interest was landscape painting. Wyeth married in 1906 and moved to Chadds Ford, Pennsylvania, where he lived until the end of his life. Chadds Ford became the center of Wyeth's personal and pictorial universe. He had a large creative family which included his son Andrew who in turn became—and still is—one of America's most popular artists (Cat. No. 153). In *Farm*, Wyeth depicted the Brandywine River Valley in rural Pennsylvania close to his Chadds Ford home. The poetic landscape has a dreamlike quality due to the choice of soft, pastel colours and the animated rhythm of curving lines which are repeated in the undulating hills, winding rivers, roads, and the billowing cloud formations rolling across the sky.